AS THE SMOKE CLEARED

Based on a True Story

JOY WINTERS

LifeRich Publishing is a registered trademark of The Reader's Digest Association, Inc.

LifeRich Publishing books may be ordered through booksellers or by contacting:

LifeRich Publishing
1663 Liberty Drive
Bloomington, IN 47403
www.liferichpublishing.com
844-686-9607

Scripture quotations taken from The Holy Bible, New International Version® NIV®Copyright © 1973 1978 1984 2011 by Biblica, Inc. Used by permission. All rights reserved worldwide.

Unless otherwise indicated, all Scripture quotations are taken from the Holy Bible, New Living Translation, copyright © 1996, 2004, 2015 by Tyndale House Foundation. Used by permission of Tyndale House Publishers, Inc., Carol Stream, Illinois 60188. All rights reserved.

ISBN: 978-1-4897-3524-9 (sc)
ISBN: 978-1-4897-3523-2 (hc)
ISBN: 978-1-4897-3525-6 (e)

Library of Congress Control Number: 2021907439

Print information available on the last page.

LifeRich Publishing rev. date: 04/12/2021

I dedicate this book to my beloved siblings, never forgotten, dearly missed, and born to win. I also dedicate this book to everyone that has helped me along the way on this crippling journey. This book is in no way an avenue to point out the flaws of others but rather to be the demonstration in times of hardships.

I wrote this not to point out the controversies in my life but to point to God and how he worked through those traumatic events to show he is God.

I am so grateful to you all, and I thank you.

Therefore, since we have been justified through faith, we have peace with God through our Lord Jesus Christ, through whom we have gained access by faith into this grace in which we now stand. And we boast in the hope of the glory of God. Not only so, but we also glory in our sufferings, because we know that suffering produces perseverance; perseverance, character; and character, hope. And hope does not put us to shame, because God's love has been poured out into our hearts through the Holy Spirit, who has been given to us. You see, at just the right time, when we were still powerless, Christ died for the ungodly. Very rarely will anyone die for a righteous person, though for a good person someone might possibly dare to die. But God demonstrates his own love for us in this: While we were still sinners, Christ died for us.

(Romans 5:5–8)

CONTENTS

CHAPTER 1

Intact Umbilical Cord

For you created my inmost being; you knit me together in my mother's womb. I praise you because I am fearfully and wonderfully made; your works are wonderful, I know that full well.

—Psalm 139: 13–14

God, before I was born into a world full of pain, you took me in your hands and prepared my fragile body for an unforgettable journey I would never feel disappointed in myself for taking but rather accomplished for the sake of the one who would teach me much more than I could imagine.

Our connection affectionately attracted me to an inner part of you. I fed on the love you had for me, and when the time came for me to finally see your face, I cried joyously, not realizing you were leaving. As the wind seemed to be against you and your back was away from me, it seemed that a part of me went along with you, the part of me I felt I could have been.

I am not the one who carelessly phones a friend repetitiously, hoping that the sound of her voice might fulfill my emptiness that you created in me. Not the one who appears to be drowning in her sorrow every minute of her life because of a constant sense of incompletion. Not the one who thinks it is crazy to shed a tear because it is clearly associated with weakness. Not the one who does not let anyone in her heart without proving that he or she is worthy of that.

I have lost many outstanding friendship possibilities because people realized they couldn't get in at all. My heart received its first break when you turned, walked away, and never came back. Ever since, my heart ached from all the painful things in my short life.

They call me Grace, Grace Still. I guess that my biological mother chose that name because she knew I would need God's grace to get through the things coming my way. I barely remember my mother's face; the picture I once had of her was lost, and it seems her image has faded away. I was two the last time I saw her face and heard her voice. "I'm going to the store and I'll be right back," she said. I watched the door close and waited for her to return, but she never did. I stand every day looking at that door in my mind that will never open and allow me to see my mother again. Everyone feels that the doctor never cut the umbilical cord.

At the time of my mother's disappearance, she had already apparently given up custody of her children. Well, she was forced. Drugs had a hold on her life, and no one could release its grip. It seemed that her love for drugs was stronger than her love for her children. It was a war between her guilty pleasure and her responsibilities. I wish I had the full story on how everything went down, but being only two when it happened leaves me with a story others told me. How does a little girl decipher the truth in such a situation?

According to my aunts and uncles on my mother's side, my mother's mother was not very fond of her daughter. She was jealous of her daughter's looks, which she had given her, and her ability to attract any man she wanted with her many talents. Her mother was intimidated by the fact that despite my mother's poor choices, she had had six beautiful children.

One day, my grandmother showed up at my mother's apartment and found only me, age two, my two brothers, ages three and three months, and a sister, age four, there alone. My sister took care of us while my mother was elsewhere. My grandmother got a little upset and allowed jealousy to influence her actions, which landed us all in foster care.

CHAPTER 2

Behind Closed Doors

No one knows what really happens behind the closed doors of some foster homes, where orphaned, neglected, or delinquent children are placed. Some such households are managed by deranged individuals who fail to look past their selfish desires to care properly for foster children and give them what their biological parents could not, people who look through a mirror adjusting the focus periodically to a point that they dehumanize the children to make them feel good about themselves. Some foster parents are kindhearted people who really want to make a difference and assist those in need. Others are in it for the money the government pays them for being foster parents. It's a matter of chance for the poor foster children.

At the time, a foster home was our last choice and perhaps best option, but the government sent my sister and older brother to one foster home while I and my younger brother went to another. He and I had three meals a day, clothes, and a nice roof over our heads, but my sister and other brother did not have the same luck. They and the other foster children in their home were deprived of their meals and beaten—or what their foster parents called "spanked"—until the white meat of their flesh was visible. The spankings were indeed signs of domestic violence and child abuse, which resulted in bloody bath water and long, painful, restless nights for the two of them.

While my older siblings were fighting for their lives, my second cousin, Bella Fumbe (meaning "enslaved"), was fighting for the custody of the four of us. My mother asked her to adopt the four of us, and she did; the process took forever, but we finally moved into Auntie Bella's house.

My tiny smile began to increase, but then it started decreasing and seemed to be blown away by adverse winds. At first, everything in Auntie Bella's home went well. She had two sons—Jafar and Kenyatta (meaning "musician"), but we called him Ken. Bella and her husband, Chad (meaning "protector"), were at that point the parents of six. Holidays were filled with joy, and our birthdays were celebrated collectively to save money and because most of our birthdays were pretty close together, which was not a problem for us. The celebrations were filled with cake, candles, and lots of laughter, and I was happy. But things went wrong.

CHAPTER 3

Unleash the Monster

My aunt and her husband split up due to what seemed to be a misunderstanding that could not be forgiven. From that day on, I felt that I was surrounded by chaos, a tornado in the midst of a storm that would never let up because Auntie Bella was at that point a single parent with six children. A single mistake made by a silly woman changed our lives for the worse.

Auntie Bella always seemed frightening to me but only because she seemed lost. Something always seemed to be bothering her, but I could never pinpoint it. It was as if she realized that a dream she had had would not come true. Maybe that had something to do with her attitude toward life. Auntie Bella had dreams of becoming a professional basketball player, but no one supported her, not even her mother. Was it a family tradition that mothers easily gave up on their children, or was it just a trend that would one day end?

Jealousy ate away at her soul because her mother's attention was focused on her sister's dreams rather than on hers. She vowed to make it as a professional basketball player so that her mother would notice her, but something happened that tarnished that vow. Many things can knock us down, but deciding to get up from the ground is most important.

Auntie Bella had severely injured herself in a college basketball game, and she let this small obstacle consume her soul. Her life took a detour; she decided to seek her parents' undivided attention no matter the cost. That desire created a selfish monster that over the years totally overcame her; it was a monster apparent to everyone but herself. I guess this selfishness had cost her her marriage, and it cost her much more later on. In time, our family began to dissipate. I believed that it was selfishness on all our parts that tore us to pieces, but maybe it was something else as well.

Despite everything that was going wrong with my family, I discovered someone—a higher power—who changed my life for the best. I have always loved God with all my heart, mind, soul, and body. When anyone asked me who God was to me, I would confidently say that he was my father. God rocked me back and forth as I entered his world. I remember holding up my small King James Version Bible, you know, the one they always threw at you at county fairs, just knowing that I'd always have God in my life. I feel that disbelief in God had something to do with the laceration in my family. I stopped believing that my prayers were being answered, and I stopped believing.

Auntie Bella continued to appear selfish, and my siblings and I suffered; we all nurtured some hatred that will stick with us until we're buried. With the constant yelling and screaming about the simplest things and the abusive beatings we suffered, how could hatred ever escape our hearts?

I'll never forget three bad days in particular out of many bad days I lived through. The first one is what tore me the most because it was the first time I had felt useless. That day continues to make me love my sister as much as I do. It was because of that one day when I felt helpless that I feel bad if I don't help her with anything she wants even today. I watched my auntie torture my sister; I was unable to move, unable to go to her assistance, and that made me feel helpless.

Lily had been through a lot, and the last thing I wanted to do was make anything worse. It seemed that as the years passed, the thing I did not want to do was exactly what I did, which was to completely cripple her with my every move. I felt it was intriguing to snitch on my sister for every mistake she made. My sister looked me in the face once day and shouted through my thick skin and into my heart that I was the reason her life was so awful. She began to leave the home in search of something we all felt we were missing.

We were all incomplete, and we could not find anything that would make us feel less empty. We all needed someone to hear our souls' screams, but nobody did. Auntie Bella did not even try to find out what was bothering us because she too felt she was missing something. She searched to fulfill her emptiness in the same way my sister did—through men—but the difference was that Auntie Bella was a parent too and neglected her duties in that area of responsibility. Auntie Bella began to lash out at Lily for every little thing she did, and that lashing out became emotionally and physically violent.

My sister became my aunt's punching bag and ignited a fire in me that no one was ever able to put out. I heard the sounds of a furious giant shaking the ground. I heard a voice deep within the body of someone yearning to be free. "Help!" the voice cried, but there was silence that connected the room I was in to the room my sister was in. For a moment, time stopped, and all I could hear was my sister's shattered chest filled with overwhelming pain.

"Hold her down!" Auntie Bella yelled at the guy she was seeing at the time. Auntie Bella repeatedly punched Lily's face. The floor was stained with Lily's blood. I watched desperately wanting to do something, but I couldn't. That day, Lily became a walking corpse. Something in her died. The next morning, I woke before everyone else and tiptoed to my sister's room. I sorrowfully placed my hand on her bruises. That was a sight that has stayed with me.

My brothers despised Auntie Bella for the constant criticism and abusive acts she would subject us all to. She was always lashing out at

8

us verbally and physically. We were everything but children to her, and she was everything but our mother. That was a choice she made when she chose to show the monster in her instead of who she could have been. I was furious and fearful of my auntie's inner monster.

It later cost me my relationship with my older brother. Nathan (gift from God) is a different character, and it's hard to say if I understand his uniqueness. I love him, and I know life had hurt him. Sometimes, I fear for his life. He has allowed his troubled soul to get into trouble. He has been known to lie and steal when he is in distress. He never made the right decisions when it came to coping mechanisms. I believe it's God's love and forgiveness that has and will continue to save his life.

He was much bolder when it came to approaching Auntie Bella. One day, he got so tired of her nonsense that he fought back; it was a fight that changed his life. It was a typical school day; he and I were on the bus coming home from school; we were both in the fourth grade. Our landlord's son was riding the school bus as well. I don't know if he was in denial of who he really was; everyone considered him to be girlish, but he was oblivious to that.

Most students pushed and shoved and scrambled to the seats in the back of the bus, while I preferred to sit toward the front so I could look out the front windows and talk to the bus driver; I was sort of a geek. My favorite part of riding the bus was fantasizing about things far beyond my reach as I gazed out the window.

My brother and I got off at our usual stop, right in front of our house. He and I walked into the house not expecting anything unusual to happen. Someone knocked on the door; I thought it was one of our friends. My auntie answered the door; our landlord was there, and she looked as if a volcano were about to erupt in her. In a high-toned voice while glaring at Nathan, she said, "Your son called my son a faggot on the bus today!"

I don't know if my auntie interrogated me the way she did out of fear or if she sincerely enjoyed it. Not even looking at Nathan, she asked me, "Grace, did your brother call our landlord's son a faggot?"

I was terrified. I shook my head and truthfully said, "I don't know." Reading my soul, she screamed again, "Did your brother call our landlord's son a faggot?" I kept saying over and over that he did not, but she kept digging and digging away at me. I wondered why she was attacking me and growling at me like a hound dog. It seemed that everything always came down to my response, so once I realized I couldn't escape reality, I gave her the answer she was looking for—"Yes"—though I knew it wasn't true.

That time and every other time I gave my auntie the answer she was looking for, it seemed I was choosing her over my own blood. My siblings hated me for that, but I was just trying to survive; I was just scared. I had been in the front of the bus and had not heard my brother say anything to our landlord's son, but she bullied me into saying yes. I can still hear her voice, a disturbing, ringing noise that will never go away. I was panicked and anxious due to her incessant questioning, and I wanted to escape her yelling. My tears meant nothing to her.

"Nathan!" my auntie exclaimed, "go downstairs, strip off all your clothes, and get ready for a beating." She professed her deepest apologizes to our landlord and walked her out the front door.

That was the last day my brother lived with us. He left and never came back. I never really knew much about my auntie's two children, but I did know that they too left the house at young ages. Jafar and Ken were not bad children; they just weren't self-driven, and just like most motherless children, they were easily defeated. They walked with their heads down.

A person never really understands the value of a parent's support until he or she is without it. Auntie Bella's lack of support had given her sons the mindset to just throw in the towel when things did not go as planned. They didn't know that nothing ever goes as planned and that it took strength to make the best of awful situations.

CHAPTER 4

Self-Blame

My family was falling apart, and it seemed that it was entirely my fault. I had snitched on my brother and was the cause of my sister's running away. It was my fault that they had eventually wound up in the state's hands. It was also my fault that Jafar and Ken had left because if it had not been for me, they might have had their mother's support.

My mind was torn with confusion, and my heart was shattered. After everything with Nathan happened, Auntie Bella decided to pack up all our stuff and leave. I don't know the real reason she decided to move, but she said, "There are too many homosexuals around this neighborhood, and I'm tired of Georgia. We're moving to Florida." I had to leave behind some of the greatest friends I had ever made. Something told me that we weren't moving because of homosexuals; over the years, moving like that had become a trend. A new area or place meant a new beginning, an erasing of all that had happened, but how many new beginnings does a person need?

Auntie Bella always had an excuse, but the only one that made sense to me was the one she used the first time we moved. That was when we moved from a standard-sized white and green house in Huntsville, Alabama, by my favorite elementary school, Heart-Shaped Elementary. She exclaimed, "I'm ready for a change, and there will be no more beatings."

There were changes, but not the type one might agree with. We kept moving and moving as our family decreased and decreased. We must have moved to five or ten different places. It was even worse after the bulk of her audience passed away, meaning her mother. I have no doubt that Auntie Bella loved her mother, but her desire to please her mother was what killed her. When her mother passed, the little part of Auntie Bella that was sane passed along with her. We children in Auntie Bella's house stood no chance against her wounded soul. Well, maybe for her biological children there was some chance, but as far as we adopted children were concerned, not so much. Apparently, the truth was that she had never wanted to adopt us; she did so only because of her mother. Why am I not surprised?

We moved from all over Huntsville, Alabama, a part of Birmingham, and from there all over Daytona, Florida, hoping for change. At least I was. I was attending Settling Middle School, the worst middle school with the worst children I had ever met. The children there were so cruel, and they were filled with unspeakable hatred. They would shout harsh comments left and right: "Hey, Grace! You're the ugliest girl in the world!" They pushed and shoved me in the halls and constantly nagged me.

One day, I was in typing class minding my own business and completing an assignment. I always sat in front in my classes because I felt that the closer I sat to the teacher, the safer I would be from the other students. The teacher was walking around the class assuring that everyone was completing the assignment and not veering off to other sites, of which most were banned anyway, when I felt something hit the back of my head. I turned around and saw that someone had thrown a computer mouse pad at me. I was stunned that the teacher had not seen that, and then it happened again. I looked back and saw two girls smirking at me. I could have said something to them and the teacher; I could have walked out of the class, but I slid down in my chair and ignored them.

I missed my older siblings. No one had stepped on me when they attended the same school I did, but then, I had to fend for myself. I was not a fighter. I was a quiet little sixth grader focusing on getting the best grades I could. I had long, black, curly hair, beautiful brown eyes with thick eyelashes, and a multitude of talents—qualities that apparently made all the sixth-grade girls hate me. They picked on me every chance they got. I guess it didn't help that I was the typical teacher's pet. I was extremely afraid of these children, and I hoped and prayed for their sake that they would leave me alone.

I started building up a tad bit of hatred for these kids, and I don't think they really wanted to bother the bundled-up hatred I had collected over the years caused not just by them but also by my experiences with my family. But God. Every day, I prayed to God to humble me at times when children were being insensitive to me, and God gave me the strength to wake up every day, catch the bus on time, and get to school. I never missed a day. Everyone and everything around me made me miserable, but somehow, I still had hope that made me persevere.

> Therefore, since we have been justified through faith, we have peace with God through our Lord Jesus Christ, through whom we have gained access by faith into this grace in which we now stand. And we boast in the hope of the glory of God. Not only so, but we also glory in our sufferings, because we know that suffering produces perseverance; perseverance, character; and character, hope. And hope does not put us to shame, because God's love has been poured out into our hearts through the Holy Spirit, who has been given to us. You see, at just the right time, when we were still powerless,

> Christ died for the ungodly. Very rarely will anyone
> die for a righteous person, though for a good person
> someone might possibly dare to die. But God
> demonstrates his own love for us in this: While we
> were still sinners, Christ died for us.
>
> (Romans 5:1–8)

Despite my trials at school, it was my auntie's contemptuousness that landed me on the steps of what would become a big part of my life, Parkway Baptist Church. This church became more like my first home than my second. During our first few weeks there, my brother and I sat in the back with our heads down. Multiple people came up to us wondering where we had come from and tried to welcome us to the church. We remained silent, and we did not contribute much at Bible study, though I saw some of my classmates there, and that made me feel a little comfortable. However, my goal was to always remain invisible so that no one would acknowledge my existence and I could hide the scars in my heart.

It took me a few years to become comfortable with the members of the church, but eventually, I came around. One day, the pastor spoke of a love that I couldn't believe was possible. He said that a man in his early twenties carried two big sticks among his open flesh as he stumbled countless times smiling to a crowd of people he called his children. They blew kisses on the wounds they had created. His blood dripped from his body, but none of his children cared enough to clean it up. They pulled skin from his malnourished body with pricking rods. The crowd jabbed nails into his hands and feet as though he had committed the worst crime, but he was innocent.

The pastor said that this young man had endured it all for the love of his children, including me. I never knew anyone who loved me enough to take such brutality; I wanted to know this young man more. I found out his name—Jesus Christ. I felt that Jesus had shaken my hand that day, introduced himself, and wanted a great relationship with me right that moment.

Along with this amazing church, God introduced to me to something else that would keep me levelheaded. Instead of using my fists to let out my anger that had built up over the years, by following Christ, my enemies became strong acquaintances throughout middle school. Every Monday, God allowed my legs to relieve my anger. Let me explain that.

I first noticed my passion for running in eighth grade. Every time my feet touched the ground, I got an exhilaration that connected me to God. Whenever I ran, I felt his presence and heard him say how much he loved me. Everyone has a place where they meet God, and running was the place I met him.

Later, my legs took me further than I had ever imagined. I managed to escape reality pretty well, and it was all God's will I thought. But just when it seemed that everything was okay, metaphorically speaking, another fire was lit and my church began to fall apart and burn up.

CHAPTER 5

Ashes

The church began to lose members and thus tithes and donations. My home didn't feel like a home, and I was losing the church home I had created. I didn't know what to think or feel at that point.

My younger brother and I had been walking over a mile to get to this church, but soon, there wouldn't be a church to walk to. And then Auntie Bella decided we should move clear across town, and what she said always went.

Several years later, I was a freshman in high school. I was still attending Parkway, but it was quickly deteriorating. My sister was living in Florida somewhere, but nobody knew her whereabouts; she just showed up whenever. Years later, I learned that she had randomly showed up at the house to check in on me and see if I was doing okay.

I wish I could say that my sister had a nice apartment, was financially stable, and had a bright future, but after she and my older brother got out of the government's custody, they ran straight into the hands of an even darker course of life—the streets. I believe neither intentionally put their lives in harm's way, but they did. I was extremely worried and afraid for their lives, but my sister's more for some reason. The love children deserve was all my sister and older brother sought. My auntie may have always wanted to feel loved by her mother, but my siblings and I just wanted to be and feel loved by anybody.

> For God so loved the world that he gave his one and only Son, that whoever believes in him shall not perish but have eternal life.
>
> (John 3:16)

Love is not what we desire it to be. It is not the gentle touch of a mother when you are born or the sweet kiss of a spouse. It is not the approval of an earthly mother or father. It is not in the words "I love you" or in a hug. It is nothing in comparison to what we strongly desire to be in our lives daily. It is not a constant tickly feeling we get deep inside when someone makes us smile. No. Love is that one act that makes our unperfected acts of kindness seem small. It is as written in the Bible that God sent Jesus to die for us.

Jesus showed us a love with no conditions or requirements attached to it. Do not believe that we deserve his love; we do not, but he gives us his love to set us free, which is what love does. Fleshly love poses expectations that when not met disturbs our insides to the point that we feel a lack of love, which holds us captive.

Neither my brother nor my sister went looking for love in the right place. My sister's desperation landed her in jail with open wounds caused by police dogs that had chased her down as she attempted to run away and a stomach overtaken by an unborn child in her.

CHAPTER 6

What's a Young Girl to Do?

That wasn't the first time Lily got pregnant; she had had five miscarriages prior to that pregnancy. I feared for her and her unborn child's life. I was a tad upset with her for leaving me in that house to fend for myself. I feared for my life every moment. I had always thought that our bond was much better than that of two wounded souls never capable of healing, but perhaps the truth was that it was not.

We were hurting, but for some reason, our love for each other was never enough to heal us. I figured that it was because we couldn't grasp what it meant to love someone. We were blinded in our minds, and it was impossible to think of anyone other than ourselves. It's easy for me to just say that I was blinded in my mind and all, but the truth was that I wanted to understand and wanted to help her, but I just didn't know how.

She got out of jail she said because she was pregnant, but I think it was because they felt bad for unleashing dogs on a pregnant girl. She came to see me, but when she felt that my auntie did not welcome her, she went to live with her abusive Italian boyfriend.

For years, we thought he was the father of her Isaiah, but it turned out he wasn't. This caused a controversy in the household, which led to domestic violence that he inflicted on my sister. So one night, she tiptoed out of the house with her children. She was running for her life. She felt it was time to go back to her hometown, where family would willingly help her. At least that's what they told her. Nothing my family ever said held the truth. While my sister was fighting battles of her own, so was the rest of the family.

I worried about my siblings as well as myself. Unlike a normal high school student, I wasn't worried about where I would attend college; I was worried about just making it through the day. Every day seemed like another impossible struggle. Auntie Bella was extremely over the top, and my brother and I seemed to just add to her problems. She said that her current boyfriend was the cause of her distress; I never understood why they did not just end their relationship. Love can make people do crazy things. I think that if love hurts, it isn't love. They argued day and night. Sometimes, they would keep my brother and me up, and we would go to school extremely exhausted.

Those long, disruptive years they were together made me vow to never be in any relationship that involved such bickering. If a woman curses you out, breaks the windshield of your car, and hits you upside the head with a combination lock sending you to the hospital, don't bother her because she might be crazy.

Her boyfriend was crazy for coming back to my auntie time after time; I never figured out why he did. I suppose that when a man's only place to turn back to is his mother's house, it is easy to come back to a place where he could feel a little good about his life.

CHAPTER 7

We Are Responsible for Our Actions

People tend to point fingers at others for their faults, but it takes a real good person to own up to his or her faults.

> The man said, "The woman you put here with me—she gave me some fruit from the tree, and I ate it."
>
> (Genesis 3:12)

Auntie Bella can blame her abusive mother, her missing out on an opportunity of a lifetime due to an injury, or her boyfriends and ex-husband, but in reality, she had control over her life, and she could have lived it differently. From Adam and Eve on, we have had free will. It is up to us to choose according to God's will for us. It was God's will for Adam and Eve not to eat of the fruit of the Tree of Knowledge of Good and Evil, but they chose to be disobedient.

It is so easy for us to slip out of God's hands and into the hands of disobedience rather than staying on the path he sets out for us that will lead us out of captivity and to peace. My auntie was being held captive but did not know that. She chose to be the person everyone saw. I don't think she realizes how awful she was to those around her and that her words built up hate in those whose lives she touched including me.

Perhaps all six of her children, those she adopted and those she gave birth to, still believe that one day she'll actually live up to the promise she once made to change for the better. It was not the disbelief I had in her that allowed me to stay and tolerate such vulgar behavior all those years. I loved her, and I will always love her. I just wish she could look at me rather than through me as if I weren't there. I should have known better after watching her allow all my siblings and her two sons to walk away from her life. It helped me realize that I was no different from the others and that she would let me go just as easily too. Even my younger brother left before I did; the time will come for you to hear that part of my story.

CHAPTER 8

Hair

Therefore I tell you, do not worry about your life,
what you will eat or drink; or about your body, what
you will wear. Is not life more than food, and the
body more than clothes?
—Matthew 6:25

When I was in tenth grade, my auntie felt it was time for me to
change my hair style. For years, I had slicked my hair back in a
nice, neat ponytail. I loved my hair. It was naturally curly when it
hit water, and unlike the hair of most African American children
my age, it was long. Her problem with my hair was how tangled it
could get, but that didn't bother me. I can't count the number of
hair dryers, the kind with combs attached, that I broke trying to
get my hair straight and manageable. I'd get frustrated when I did
my hair; I wasn't one of those perky young girls who enjoyed doing
her hair. I simply would rather be doing anything else. That is why
I kept my hair in braids.

But braids weren't good enough for my auntie being the controlling woman she was. She thought that getting my hair relaxed a bit would better suit me. She always compared her hair to mine, and hers came out worse in her mind. She was jealous of me, but how could anyone be jealous of her child? I felt that she was trying to do with my hair what she wished she could do with hers. It was as though I had become her toy doll. For years, I told her I never wanted a perm because I loved my hair the way it was, and everyone knew that if you got a perm, you would risk losing all your hair if you didn't maintain it. Later, I realized through one of her harsh comments that my losing my hair had been a part of her evil scheme. She really was out to destroy us.

With spit flying from her mouth, she threatened me about getting a relaxer. She maliciously darted discouraging words at me. "Grace," she said, "you look like complete crap, and I'm tired of having to look at you." She drove me to a beauty salon, and when I did not get out of the car, she came around to the passenger's door stomping the ground like an earthquake and yelled, "Grace! Get out of this car or I'll pull every inch of your hair out of your head."

I was in tears. She grabbed my wrist squeezing it as tight as a wire and dragged me into the salon. I went in as myself and came out as the young girl she wanted me to be. That day, I realized that my life was in the hands of a woman with a monster inside her. Grinding her teeth as she jabbed the key into the ignition, she said, "Grace, if you even think about putting your hair in a ponytail, I'll beat you until your blood seeps through your clothes, so don't try me." With my voice cracking with fear, I said, "Yes ma'am." People say a person cannot make you do anything, but she could hypnotize me into doing anything.

There were days when my hair would fly in front of my face and I would reach up to swat it away, but my auntie's voice would blow my hand away with the constant reminder of her threat. I was miserable. I did not know what to do, but feeling as I did, I wanted to fight back.

One day, my brother Josiah, my auntie, and I were walking around my high school at my tenth-grade orientation. Booths were set up for the different things my high school had to offer that year, and the swim team had a booth. I thought that my hair would be ruined if I took up swimming; that was how I could get back at my auntie and stop feeling miserable.

"Auntie Bella, can I join the swim team?" I asked.

Without a thought, she said, "Sure. I don't care." Though I wanted to join the swim team to get back at her, I would have liked her to show her support for me by coming to at least one of my meets. She made excuses after excuses for her absence. I don't know why I ever expected her to actually show up to one of my swim meets; she never supported any of her children with anything they did. Wasn't that what our mother should have done?

At least I had my team and my coaches; they would be the support I needed.

CHAPTER 9

Discovering My Talent

My time on the swim team didn't last long. One moment helped me realize I could excel at a different sport. One day after a long and exhausting swim practice, I challenged one of the males on my team to race me on foot. Maybe God was putting his plan for me into action that day. I was the slowest swimmer on the team, but I could run fast. When I would race my brothers, they would give up before the end so that they would not have to admit I was faster than them. Typical prideful males.

My teammate and I started our race behind the bleachers that were facing the pool. A gate way out in front of us would be our stopping point. The first step is always the hardest and the most important one. That step would determine if I would win. That step would determine my boldness. That step would be the start of my future. Everything my life stood for was counting on my taking that step. I had been waiting for this moment for a long time, but I hadn't realized it.

We stepped up to the starting line we had created, and as everyone on our swim team watched, a teammate yelled, "Go!" We were off. The feeling was incredible I raced in confidence that I had him beat. I had my eyes on the prize the whole time, but it didn't dawn on me that I was actually winning until we were only steps away from the finish line.

Confidence can take you further than you might ever know. I had won with the entire swim team as my witnesses. For once in my life, I had won something. In a world of losers, I was a winner. That gave me hope, but I also acknowledged the gift God had given me—the passion to become fast. I smiled, shook my teammate's hand, and walked away from swimming.

I was afraid my auntie would not want me to run. It's always hard to ask for something you really want; at least that's the case with me. Who wants to hear no when it involves something you really want to do? It's like a child opening Christmas presents but not finding the one he or she really wanted—just a bunch of clothes and shoes. So like a coward, I asked my little brother Josiah to ask my auntie for me, and he did. My little brother was not afraid of anything; at least that's how he acted. He could not understand why I was so afraid of our auntie, a mere mortal.

Josiah asked our auntie that night if I could join the track team, and she said, "Yes, but she should know I won't be supporting her." I didn't care. I was just relieved that she had said yes.

The next day after school, I asked the running coaches if I could be on the team. In their eyes, I saw that they had no great expectations for me, but they didn't know that I had talent. Actually, I had no idea that I had talent. I set off with the help of my church family to earn the money I needed to be a part of the team, a team that became a family I created for myself.

CHAPTER 10

Perseverance

Be joyful in hope, patient in affliction, faithful in
prayer.
—Romans 12:12

My life was about to begin without my truly realizing it. I was
grateful that I would have a place to be besides home. I had practice
every day after school, and it usually ran late, which left little to no
time for homework, but somehow or another, I made it all work.

In high school, half the time, I wasn't aware of what I was doing;
I was just going through the motions, but every once in a while, I
woke up from my countless daydreams; it was as though I were on
drugs that allowed me to escape my dreadful life. My auntie's voice
was the poison I so desperately wanted out my body and brain.

What people don't know is that they can trap themselves with
drugs, alcohol, and sex. I hadn't wanted that poison in my life, and
I wanted it out completely, not just temporarily. I did whatever it
took to be successful on the track team. No matter how much anger

I had built up in me from the lack of care I experienced at home, I was determined to make it.

One day, I walked two hours to run five miles and then walked two hours to get back home. I was dedicated. After a while, my coaches caught on to my lack of transportation and started giving me rides home, but I felt bad about that. It wasn't as if my auntie wasn't able to pick me up; she just wouldn't.

Josiah fell very ill, but my auntie refused to take him to the doctor for his eczema cream. Just as she didn't become involved in my life, she refused to be involved in his life even if that could have meant his death.

Every day, I opened his door, checked on him, and prayed to God for his help. I was afraid Josiah was going to die. All I could do was pray and keep asking my auntie to take him to the hospital. She looked at me in disgust and said, "He doesn't take showers. That's why he's sick." She didn't know that he had developed a staph infection in his blood that could have killed him. I saw in her eyes that she was totally uninterested in helping her son.

She finally agreed to take him to the hospital; once again, God answered my prayers. Sadly, Josiah had been out of school for over a month, which caused him to fail and flunk out. Every day, I would open his door and looked into the eyes of a young man who had been defeated due to helplessness despite my attempt to encourage him to stay strong. He was not the only one who felt helpless. Was there more that I could have done at that time? I wasn't sure, but I watched my brother suffer from something he shouldn't have had to. How could any mother deny her child a necessary trip to the hospital? She was a stranger rather than a mother to us; she had given up her right to be considered our mother.

By the grace of God, my brother's life was spared, and he was ready to move on with his life. Every once in a while, Josiah stayed after school to make up the work he had missed over the month he was sick. He too was dedicated to succeeding. One day, my brother's ride fell through and he needed a lift home. I asked my coach if he could take us both home, and just as always, he said yes but in two hours. My brother got angry not at my coach but at our auntie, who refused to have anything to do with us. As far as my brother was concerned, she was going to pick us up whether she liked it or not.

Over the years, my brother developed a low tolerance for ignorance, and once he was fed up with a situation, nothing could stop him from voicing his opinion on it. He called our auntie and asked her to pick us up. My brother was angry, but he didn't let his troubled heart triumph over his good character; he was extremely polite when talking with our auntie. She pulled up, and her look was that of someone who was extremely angered that she had to take care of us.

My brother and I started getting in the back seat, but she demanded that I sit in front, so I hesitantly did so. The ride home was like a silent film that somehow gained sound after my auntie threw her phone at Josiah's face and started punching his face; he just sat back and crossed his arms in defiance and defense. Eventually, his humbleness caused my auntie to stop in the middle of the road and to insist that he get out. As my brother exited the car with blood running down his face, my auntie yelled, "I don't deserve this! I'll kill you both!"

My eyes filled with tears. My brother and I did not deserve such treatment, but I was too frightened to say anything. Like a coward, I drove home with what I has concluded was an awful creature. My life was beginning to look like the Jordan River on the day God was trying to tell Pharaoh to let his people go by filling the river with blood of creatures that resembled my auntie.

Right after my auntie and I got home, a police car pulled up. An officer from school demanded that we go back to school to explain what was going on with my brother. I knew my auntie felt guilty for what she had done and said. Part of me felt that she didn't mean to hurt my brother, but bad deeds are punished. My auntie and I got back to school, and the police officer approached my auntie's car and told us to go to the front office.

In the office, she told the officer, "I was having a discussion with Josiah and not knowing my phone was in my hand, I reached back, and it slipped out of my hand" fully confident that her words were the truth. "Officer," she exclaimed, "Josiah has always had a temper, which in this case caused him to irrationally jump out of my vehicle and walk back to school. I decided to leave him here only until he cooled off."

I was in awe that she would twist the truth to blame her child, whom she had intentionally insulted and harmed. The officer asked me, "Is this true, Grace? Did your aunt accidentally drop her phone on your brother's face?" For once, I did not give the answer my auntie had expected. "No," I exclaimed. "My auntie threw her phone at my brother and punched him several times as he sat back and did nothing." I couldn't look at my auntie, but I thought that for once, she felt defeated.

"Ma'am," the officer exclaimed, "you're under arrest for assaulting your son. You have the right to remain silent. Anything you say can be held against you in the court of law."

I should have felt relieved, but I felt awful. I felt defeated. My brother and I were taken out of my auntie's home and placed in what I thought was a permanent home, but it turned out to be a temporary place.

CHAPTER 11

Wishing I Could Escape My Mind

I thought that was goodbye, but for some reason, Florida soon put us back with our auntie. We were all required to have family counseling separately and together. What could we hope for? Did we really not love each other? What is love? What was internally eating away at us that caused this bitterness? No one could answer my questions.

My auntie was charged with assault and battery on a minor because my brother irritably pressed charges. That gave her another reason to look down on him, which in time led him to leave her house for good. He was gone just like that, and I was stuck just like that.

The beatings were all a part of life. The yelling and sudden outbursts were all a part of the hurt eating away at my auntie. As a child of God, I wanted to forgive her, but I continued to have trouble. The confusion sent me into a deep and dark tunnel of depression that I was afraid I would never get out of. I was constantly battling in my mind about the purpose of my life. My friends on my running team and my classmates began to worry as I continued to hurt and desperately cried out for help. I looked as if I were struggling with anorexia. Every night, my mind would wander to the same dream over and over.

My brain had planned my death. The thoughts were due to my auntie's lack of interest in my life. As a result of my dream, I wanted to make sure she was the one who found my body in my room. I had an old, rusty knife with which I would stab myself in the stomach for a slow fade from this world. This would give me enough time to place letters I had in a specific manner. I would then lie against the wall and gaze at the doorknob hoping it would turn and open with my auntie behind it.

As she opened the door and headed toward my quivering body, she would finally see me for me. Barely being able to move. I would hand her a multitude of goodbye letters I had written to those I loved. She would ignore my letters, and I would let them fall to the floor. She would scramble to the phone to call an ambulance.

But by the time the paramedics arrived, it would be too late. Auntie would pick up the stack of letters, and the one for her would be on top. She would read it; it would contain my wish for my family to be together and my desperate apology for tearing us apart. I would die knowing finally that she actually cared about me; her tears would say it all. I would finally know that she was willing to help me, but I would be beyond help.

As I woke each night from this devastating dream, I felt that if this dream actually happened, she might listen to my wish. I concluded that no wish was worth all that trouble, so in the end, I told myself to never act on such an idea.

I also realized that bundling everything up inside wasn't good because at some point if I wasn't careful, I'd end up taking my life as a good friend of mine had. Isaac (which means he laughs, laughter) was the son of a preacher, a single parent, who smiled everywhere he went. He brought joy to so many people including me. He was a red-headed, freckle-faced kid just as sweet as honey. I had never met anyone with such enthusiasm for life. That is why no one saw the end of his life coming.

Sorrow had built up in him to such an extent that he killed himself with his father's gun. I cried and mourned over the loss of this wonderful friend. You can't judge a book by its cover. This was so hard on his family and friends. The day I attended his funeral, I vowed to never think of suicide again. I was ready to work on living.

CHAPTER 12

The Gateway to My Heart

My auntie and Josiah continued to have disputes until finally he found himself out of my auntie's house and living in a home for children who did not have anywhere else to go. It was similar to a foster home. The couple who were the house parents loved him so much that they wanted to adopt him. You can imagine how they felt when they found out he had been adopted by someone who didn't want anything to do with him.

His new home was way across town. I was alone defending myself in a house where all I had was God and running. I spent as much time as I could after school training and running. I was focused, but that was until I met a guy I couldn't help but fall in love with. To some extent, I believed meeting him was a mistake. I looked into his eyes as we shook hands, and I just knew he was the one.

Jariel (meaning strong, open minded) was his name, and he was a junior who had transferred from West Palm Beach, Florida, where he had grown up with his father and stepmother. My mind was in a tug-of-war with the idea of a romantic relationship, running track, making excellent grades, and having a successful future. Stubborn and determined as always, I worked on having it all. But I was hesitant to begin a relationship with Jariel; for one thing, I wasn't sure if he felt the same way about me as I did about him, not until he started showing interest in our becoming somewhat of a couple.

He was on my running team had just finished a race in Panama City, one of the most beautiful places in Florida known for lovely beaches. On the drive back from the race, we held hands, and he told me in a flirtatious manner about how nice mine were. The moment was magical.

The next day, I confronted him with how I was feeling about the two of us naively believing I couldn't live without him. I was finally ready to let someone in my heart and be a part of my life. I was confident and ready as I approached him and blurted out, "I have a crush on you, and I'd really like to be your girlfriend."

He tilted his head and said something I had not been expecting: "I have a girlfriend I've been dating for a year and a half."

Baffled, furious, and embarrassed, I asked, "Why have you been so flirtatious if you had no interest in being with me romantically?"

Confidently, he said, "I wasn't being flirtatious. I was just being polite."

I was bursting with rage. "What do you call holding hands on a two-hour ride back from Panama City? Do you call that being polite?"

He just nodded. How could he expect me to believed he was just being polite? Surely he knew I would begin to have feelings for him if he held my hand that long. I should have stopped even thinking of him after that, but young love makes a person do crazy things. I was upset that Jariel had led me on and then denied having feelings for me.

Most important, I was upset that he couldn't be mine. I wish I could say I just let it all go and decided to move on, but I had realized that he had an easily influenced mind, and I decided to take advantage of that. That's what I planned while I rehearsed in front of my bedroom mirror, but being a child of God, I decided that wasn't the smartest or the most Christian thing to do.

The next week, we decided to just be friends and put everything behind us, but that was hard for me; I looked into his eyes every day at running practice. I felt I was falling deeper and deeper in love with him. It's crazy what hormones can do to a person; thinking about it now, I realize I was in lust, not love, with Jariel.

After practice one day, I saw that he looked a little under the weather. He had my full attention when I asked him, "Hey Jariel, why the long face?"

He couldn't look me in the eye when he said, "Grace, my girlfriend broke up with me last night."

For some reason, I felt relieved because perhaps I had persuaded her to leave him so he could be with me, but how could that be possible? I'd never spoken to the girl. Despite my feelings for him, I maintained my concerning posture and asked, "Umm, and how does that make you feel?"

He started off every statement with, "Well, to be honest ..." He said it hurt because he truly wanted things to work out between us. "I really care about her."

"Jariel, if you truly care and want to be with her, despite it being a long-distance relationship, tell her that's how you feel." In disbelief, I wondered why I had just given the guy I liked advice to go be back with his ex-girlfriend. He nodded and thanked me for listening.

The next day, Jariel and his ex were back together, and ironically, I had had something to do with it. I guess I really wasn't the type to break up a relationship.

Days later, Jariel and his girlfriend separated again, but that time, it was his own doing. It might have had something to do with a certain question I had asked him during a track meet three days earlier. I walked to the track early Saturday morning around 7:30, and the coaches had just begun setting up for track and field championships hosted by our high school. I was hoping Jariel would be there, and he came. My face lit up with joy.

Jariel, I, and my best friend on the team were assigned to handle the same work station at the meet. I tried to not flirt with him, but that was impossible. His eyes hypnotized me. His eyes spoke of his innocence; as I gazed into them, I saw a glimpse of me in him. He looked like a child in search of the type of joy that brought tears to your eyes. I thought that he might understand the lost child in me. I yearned for a connection with someone else who understood pain, and I thought love would triumph over pain.

Jariel and I talked that day and got to know each other better. My best friend on the other hand wasn't having the greatest night because he was upset that I was focusing my attention on Jariel. Quick lesson here—When beginning a romantic relationship, don't forget about others in your life. I was indeed focused just on Jariel. What would happen if things didn't work out between us? I would have let go of everyone who loved and cared for me. I was determined to not let that happen, so I made room for everyone.

At sunset, Jariel and I began to get restless, so we decided to go for a jog without being relieved of our duties. When we returned, the meet was almost over. I looked into his eyes examining his heart as he looked into my eyes feeding on his curiosity of who I was. I put a hand on his shoulder and said, "I know what I want." I moved my hand to his chest. "Listen to your heart and figure out what you want."

He gently took my hand as we gazed into each other's eyes and smiled. He leaned closer to me and said goodnight. I sighed and walked away anticipating the next time I would see him.

CHAPTER 13

Open Wounds

Love is patient and kind. Love is not jealous or boastful or proud or rude. It does not demand its own way. It is not irritable, and it keeps no record of being wronged. It does not rejoice about injustice but rejoices whenever the truth wins out. Love never gives up, never loses faith, is always hopeful, and endures through every circumstance.
> —1 Corinthians 13:4–7 (NLT)

The love I felt for Jariel was nothing about which the scriptural passage above spoke. I wasn't patient, so I forced a love that was set up to fail. When a person rushes a relationship, it screams chaos. I take all the blame for wanting something Jariel and I were unsure about.

The relationship was going great until we ran into a huge disagreement. Jariel wanted to be more intimate—he wanted to have sex. Personally and spiritually, I wanted to wait until marriage. I was already intimate with God, and I had promised God I would wait to be intimate with anyone else until the day he was ready to give me away to a strong, faithful man.

If I hadn't been a virgin and Jariel hadn't tasted physical intimacy with other women, maybe our relationship would have flourished, but instead, it got tarnished. Behind Jariel's innocent eyes was someone I grew to resent. I was disgusted. How could something so right one moment seem so wrong the next moment? Intimacy ... I had my reasons for not wanting that ...

Years before, I had pleaded with the Lord to forgive my young body. I was only a child who did not know much, but still, I believed it was all my fault. I had not said no and had not said stop; in a way, it was as if I had wanted it. I became someone I never wanted to be; at least that's how I experienced this disgusting act that would erupt once it was known to the world.

I was scared as silence overwhelmed my child's body. I became confused as he whispered in my ears what he wanted. He told me that he was jealous and that I was his alone. I was only seven, and he was twenty-five. It all started one night when he tiptoed into my room and exclaimed that he wanted to sleep next to me, but as I was asleep, he fondled me. The same disgust I had for that man from age seven to twelve was the same disgust I had for Jariel. I had asked God for forgiveness for such a discouraging act before, and I wasn't going to keep revisiting that shame by settling with the idea and truth that God forever forgives.

It's crazy how many times people jump into something only to find themselves drowning because people refused to save them. I jumped into this relationship with Jariel and drowned. I'd taken so many leaps in my life, and the only one who had been there for me was my heavenly father. God was the only one faithful to me, and because of that, I chose to be faithful to him.

People will stab you in the back, and it might take years for the knife to actually come out and the wound to heal if it ever does because the person who stabbed you just keeps reopening it. My wounds are always fresh because I allow them to be. Jariel cut in and out of the wound he placed upon me for years.

Intimacy can be a drug; once you've tasted its bittersweet, satisfying pleasure, it's hard to stop wanting more. Jariel was addicted too. It seemed that everyone around me became addicted to something, and if we are not careful, everything around us becomes a drug.

I loved Jariel and wanted to be with him, but because of my past and the promise I made to God, the leap I took was just too shallow, and the relationship was over. I asked him, "Can we just be friends?" because I had false hope. Love is when there is a strong connection between two people, and it's worth fighting for only when it's true love.

Jariel once told me that I didn't know how to love, and due to my past experiences, I could agree with that, but who truly knows what love is besides God? Jariel and I were too young to grasp love's true definition. People twice our age couldn't do that, and he and I were not about to outsmart the world.

What was done was done; we were just not meant to be. As my relationship with Jariel crumbled, so did my heart. For years, I had dreamed of escaping the walls of misery in my auntie's house. I was ready to leave her home but had no idea how to until Nathan one Christmas holiday introduced me to the Duncan family. It wasn't easy for me to just walk away from the disasters in my life, but it was time for me to do that. I was tired of feeling unsafe at home, feeling that I was a stranger there. I was tired of not feeling that she cared about me, or loved me, or even listened to me.

The Duncan family was a well-off African American family consisting of three daughters, a son, who was the youngest of the four, and a happily married husband and wife. It all began when my brother introduced me to his girlfriend, their oldest daughter. The first time I met her and her family, I really wasn't interested in being a part of their lives for long. The Duncans seemed to enjoy rubbing their riches in people's faces. My brother and his girlfriend were doing well in their relationship, so I didn't question that situation too much. Despite how well the relationship was going, Nathan wasn't staying with this family; he was staying with a hardworking couple who were also well off—extremely successful. My older brother had a roof over his head, food, and a family that was serious about his success. For once, he was actually doing okay. For a short time in his life, Nathan was making all the right choices.

CHAPTER 14

The Duncan Family

I was dying inside due to the lack of concern my auntie had for me. Over the course of a few months, I established a close relationship with the Duncans as they became aware of the problems I was having at home. The Duncans and I agreed that maybe it would be best if I moved in with them. I practically had already moved in as I was spending most of my days and nights in their home.

I was only seventeen then, still a minor, and I was looking forward to graduating from high school and attending the University of Florida, whose athletic department had offered me a track and field scholarship. My future was looking bright. I had given the monsters in my life seventeen years of my life but had somehow survived all that.

"Go ahead, sweetie. Do what your heart has to do," Mrs. Duncan told me as we pulled up to my house. I climbed out and went into the vacant house. I packed up all my belongings and ran back to the car. "Hurry!" Mrs. Duncan's daughters told me.

"Help me!" I said fearing my auntie could show up at any minute and try to stop me. I got in the car and never looked back. I felt I was finally free. The Duncans and I drove off feeling relieved. It was over.

My phone began to vibrate. I looked at the caller ID. Sure enough, it was my auntie. Naively, I answered hoping she was calling to talk about something other than all my things suspiciously missing from the room I had once felt trapped in. "Hello?"

"Where are your things?" she yelled.

"They're gone along with me."

"Are you with that Duncan family?" she asked furiously.

"Yes."

"If you don't come back, I'll call the police and tell them they kidnapped you!"

I didn't know what to say, so I hung up.

She called back and demanded, "Where do they live?"

I looked at Mrs. Duncan and told her what my auntie wanted to know. She told me to give her their address and said they had nothing to be afraid of, so I did.

At the Duncan home, we heard *Thump!* on the door. Mrs. Duncan gracefully answered. Without being invited, my auntie barged in and demanded, "Where's Grace?"

Mrs. Duncan called me to the living room where she, Mr. Duncan, my auntie, and her best friend were. Looking around the Duncan's home, she said, "I see why you don't want to come home."

I was silent. I had forgotten how well off the Duncans were. Money, riches, and massive houses meant nothing to me. Had this couple been different and not willing to listen to my troubled spirit, I would have passed them by as I had done many others. I never took a single thing from the Duncans; in fact, I strove to give back to them as a symbol of my gratitude.

I finally looked at my auntie and said, "No, it isn't because of why you think."

She leaned toward me as though she were ready to bite me and yelled, "Who do you think you are talking to me like that?"

Mrs. Duncan said, "Grace, go to the dining room and let us adults talk."

I ran off grateful that Mrs. Duncan had saved me from my auntie's claws. I sat in the dining room with discouragement written all over my face. I wanted to scream. A part of me felt that I had been wrong to leave her, but another part of me felt I deserved to be treated better. I wasn't sure I was playing the cards God dealt me right. I was lost.

"I don't deserve this! I never wanted them anyway!" were the last words my auntie blurted out. She stomped out of the Duncans' home. Just like that, she was gone.

CHAPTER 15

Completely Torn

Even if I should choose to boast, I would not be a
fool, because I would be speaking the truth. But
I refrain, so no one will think more of me than is
warranted by what I do or say, or because of these
surpassingly great revelations. Therefore, in order
to keep me from becoming conceited, I was given a
thorn in my flesh, a messenger of Satan, to torment
me. Three times I pleaded with the Lord to take it
away from me.

—2 Corinthians 12:6–8

Things were finally changing for me; for once, I was with people
who loved me and saw me for who I was. Or did they? For some
reason, I found it hard to adapt to this new home after having
gotten used to living a certain way. I was torn between belonging
there versus belonging at my auntie's; my spirit wasn't settled, but I
focused on my future.

I graduated from high school, and the Duncans saw me off to my first year of college. Things seemed to be going well. I was ecstatic to be able to call someone mother and her to act like one. I was joyous, but I still felt some guilt.

One day, I called Mrs. Duncan wanting to tell her how I felt.

"Hello, Grace! How's school?"

"School's great, Mrs. Duncan. I'm just trying to get the hang of the transition from high school to college."

"Great to hear, sweetheart. So what's on your mind?"

"Well, I'm not sure how I feel about my leaving my auntie the way I did. I mean, she's technically my mother."

Mrs. Duncan sighed. "That's true. All I can say is if you feel so strongly about her, why don't you try working it out with her?"

"I don't know, Mrs. Duncan."

"Just think about it, okay, sweetheart?"

"Thanks, Mrs. Duncan. I will. I have to go to class now. Thanks for talking with me. Love you."

"Anytime. Love you too."

I did think about it. I also prayed to the Lord about what I should do. As I was walking to class, I read a sign, "What Are Your Plans for Christmas Break?" I knew that I would have to leave campus during the semester break, and I thought I could spend some of those days with my auntie and the rest with the Duncans. I texted Mrs. Duncan about that, but I never heard back from her.

During the break, I was at my auntie's when Mrs. Duncan called me. "Where are you, Grace?"

"Mrs. Duncan, I'm at my auntie's. Didn't you get the text I sent you a while back?"

"What text? I never received any text! If you want to stay there, go ahead, but don't plan on coming back here!"

I was in shock feeling that someone had ripped my heart out. What had I done? I dreamed about the Duncans all the time; whenever I saw their family portrait I had in my dorm room, I imagined being in the picture. Yes, I had messed up. It's just like people to be unreliable. The Duncans did the one thing I'd been unable to do—trust in God fully. I had trusted my instincts, and they had given me human results. I'd been thrown out into the world alone to live with my regrets. I'd felt guilty ever since I'd left my auntie even though doing so had given me a fresh start, a new season of life.

I could never be Mrs. Duncan's daughter or her daughters' sister; I just wanted to be their friend. They had believed in me and trusted me, but I had messed up. They had been there for my eighteenth birthday and my high school graduation and prom, and they had accompanied me to freshman orientation. They had filled the emptiness in my heart, and I had just pulled the plug and caused a leak emptying my heart again.

The Duncans were supposed to be my family, the family I had always wanted. But only part of me was in the Duncan household; another was with my auntie. She wasn't very artistic when it came to depicting herself as a mother through her actions, but I had a vision of my auntie one day living up to the documents she had signed to get custody of me. She wasn't always mean to me; every once in a while, the person I knew she was showed up. I understood her reasoning for distancing herself from her children even if they couldn't. It wasn't until she actually left by placing herself under the deceitful armor of the monster in her that I realized I was truly alone. She had a piece of me I would never get back.

I thought it was impossible to replace my auntie as my mother, but I tried. At that point, I wanted Mrs. Duncan to be my mother, but one mistake I had made had allowed the opportunity to slip through my fingers. Everything seemed to be falling to pieces. I wondered how I could have done things better.

CHAPTER 16

Her vs. Him

I've realized that neither my auntie nor Mrs. Duncan could have ever been my mother. The soul of my biological mother was lost in so much more than drugs and a troubled past consisting of neglect, violence, and the incapacity to love.

I had no mother. I never would have one. It took me a long time to understand what I had deprived myself of due to the absence of a mother. For the majority of my short-lived life, I had tried to make sense of why my mother didn't want anything to do with me. That became my main focus. I'd always had this vivid picture of what I would have liked for her to be like. I pictured her as loving, nurturing, caring, and supportive; I pictured her reading to me and my falling asleep in her arms. I created my mother, but instead of actually living with her, she was just six letters—Mother.

God, however, was with me daily: "Yet to all who did receive him, to those who believed in his name, he gave the right to become children of God" (John 1:12). He was my father, someone who would never leave me. I wanted to be brave enough to remain steadfast in everything the Lord had given me. My current life reminded me of a Bible story.

A man in the crowd answered, "Teacher, I brought you my son, who is possessed by a spirit that has robbed him of speech. Whenever it seizes him, it throws him to the ground. He foams at the mouth, gnashes his teeth and becomes rigid. I asked your disciples to drive out the spirit, but they could not." "You unbelieving generation," Jesus replied, "how long shall I stay with you? How long shall I put up with you? Bring the boy to me." So they brought him. When the spirit saw Jesus, it immediately threw the boy into a convulsion. He fell to the ground and rolled around, foaming at the mouth. Jesus asked the boy's father, "How long has he been like this?" "From childhood," he answered. "It has often thrown him into fire or water to kill him. But if you can do anything, take pity on us and help us." "If you can?" said Jesus. "Everything is possible for one who believes." Immediately the boy's father exclaimed, "I do believe; help me overcome my unbelief!"

(Mark 9:17–24)

I was living in disbelief. I was yearning for someone I could never have in my life, and I was not appreciating the one who was there for me and always would be.

CHAPTER 17

FOG—Fading away, Out of My Mind, Gone

———— ⚬⚬ ————

The eye is the lamp of the body. If your eyes are
healthy, your whole body will be full of light. But
if your eyes are unhealthy, your whole body will
be full of darkness. If then the light within you is
darkness, how great is that darkness!
                                        —Matthew 6:22–23

It seemed as though my life was moving faster than I could write
about it. My story was one of truth immersed in pain and a lack of
love. What is love? Was it the computer cord pressed against my wet
skin causing permanent scars that my auntie would call tough-love
punishment? Was it the soft, gentle hand a much older man placed
on my body continuously for his pleasure? Was it out of love that
one day, I listened to him apologizing for what he had done to me
when he was twenty-five, when he was supposedly a child of God
who should have known that what he was doing to a girl was wrong?

Was it Jariel's desire to take our relationship to the next level insisting that sex was the glue we needed to make our relationship stick?

I'm not an expert on love, but I've learned that it isn't sorry or persuasive and that it most definitely does not inflict intentional pain. It took one picture to change my perception of love forever. The day I was dunked into water and raised into life with God, who graciously sent his only begotten son to die for our sins, the water was clear, but for some reason, it was later filled with dark sand, quicksand at that, and it was pulling me down.

I was twelve when I was baptized. I thought that my troubles wouldn't be washed away by baptism but that by acknowledging God as my savior, things would become better for me. Instead, it seemed as though things were getting worse. I was looking at the world from the bottom of a dirty puddle formed by the tears I cried every day. I started to forget God's love.

As the years went on, I began to dry off from God's wisdom and fall for worldly deceptions, which caused me to drift into depression, something no one could understand unless they had experienced it. At times, I would drift away from life into a daze wishing and hoping for death by imagining the worst. Depression caused me to feel I was lying on my deathbed preparing to leave this world. My body was always cold, and my stomach would growl yearning to not be neglected. It would eat away at itself, and I would begin to fade from this dreadful place called earth. I never thought I would still be trapped and immersed in the chaos of my auntie's house after being gone from it for some time. I was four hours away, but my spirit was still bothered by the awful words my auntie had said that had pierced my heart. They were leeches that were still sucking away at my heart.

If God knew how much I could bear, why did my burdens never seem as light as God said they would be? What trick was I missing to better my life?

51

CHAPTER 18

Burying Truth in Productivity

During my freshman year in college, I put my past behind me and focused on the race ahead of me. I assumed that the obstacles and hurdles I faced were just a part of life. I was juggling running practices at seven in the morning, six classes—at least two a day—and being employed for the first time in my life. Every second of every day was filled so that my mind had little if any time to ponder my regrets. Time management became my best friend. At times, it was difficult to balance everything, but I somehow did.

My relationship with God was shaky, but I was determined to keep it going. My relationship with him boomeranged every once in a while; I would distance myself from him, but then I would come right back. I knew that my relationship with God needed a lot of work, and I was ashamed I wasn't willing to work on it.

I had one roommate, and I shared a bathroom with thirty females. My college required freshmen to live in dorms, and I lived in one of cheapest dorms to save money. I lived on the third floor of Castor Hall and had a resident assistant who made us feel comfortable and safe.

I had settled into my room and was pondering my new adventure with eyes closed when someone said, "The diva has arrived!" I opened my eyes and saw a short, ginger-haired girl with the cutest freckles. She was embarrassed by her father's announcement of her arrival. I helped her bring in some of her belongings, much more than I had come with. What caught my eye was the zebra prints on everything she had brought—bedspread, sheets, suitcase, towels, boxes, and even duct tape.

"Hello," she said as she held out her hand to me. "My name's KC."

"Hi. I'm Grace. Would you like some help?"

"Naw. My dad's bringing up the last of my bags."

"Welcome to our room," I said.

She looked around. "It's so tiny."

"Yeah, they don't give you much space," I said, "but I'm sure we can make it work."

The diva had arrived. I wondered if we would get along, if our differences would make us clash. But she seemed nice, and I thought we would get along just fine. It didn't seem that she would be a problem for me; I just hoped I wouldn't be a problem for her.

College would be nothing like high school. There were no lunch bells to tell you when to eat, and there were no buses taking you where you needed to go; you had to walk, bike, or run to wherever you needed to be. There were not small classes of thirty students with teachers who took interest in you; teachers were professors, and some classes had up to two hundred students. The professors cared more about their paychecks than they did their students' education, but some did give a rat's about their students.

As a student athlete, I had track practice. Training for the season was a challenge. Transitioning from high school training to college training was not easy. At college, we athletes had to lift weights twice a week, while most high school athletes had never set foot into a weight room prior to college. My plate was full mostly with stuff I wasn't sure I could eat. Thank goodness I wasn't the only one who felt that way.

CHAPTER 19

Let the Races Begin

I had always been a runner, and for the most part, I was running toward my goal, my dream career. The feeling I got from running was one of accomplishment; that encouraged me to be persistent. What I wanted was not a selfish desire; I wanted to discover the gift God had given me—speed. I prayed that I would see God's footsteps right beside mine when I ran. He was in control and would always be if I stayed focused on him.

It wasn't until I realized that, at times, I was running away from something or someone that my goal began to seem impossible. It was either my past trailing behind me or the scary footsteps of the caretaker who had instilled fear so deep in me. Every once in a while, I would look up, and there was its shadow glaring at my soul like a sword on a mission to make me bleed.

"Take your mark!"

I snapped back to reality. I focused on the next repetitious interval my coach had created to better me as a runner.

"Go!"

Extremely determined, my coach yelled at me, "Stand three feet taller than you are, and use your arms to press forward!"

With my body tightening up, each step became harder and harder, but my coach believed in my capabilities. "Surge, Grace! Finish strong!"

I dropped my chin and did as my coach told me, finishing with all the strength I had. "Good job. Give me six more three fifties. Strive to get better and better each rep."

With every bit of the air I had left in me, I said, "Yes, Coach." I was a freshman track and field athlete in college who felt my high school coaches had not prepared me half as much as I needed to be prepared for college workouts. I felt I was dying with every rep. I loved my high school, and I was missing it desperately. Because I competed in multiple events in high school, I had had several coaches, and they had all played different roles in helping me become sort of successful, but they had shorthanded me a little bit with this one.

There was Coach James, who was always there for moral support, and that's not just because he was everyone's guidance counselor too. His last words to me were, "Your follow-through is bad." He meant that when it came to finishing things, I'd give up and never finish. Why would a counselor put down a student instead of building her up? After that, I never spoke to him again.

Then there was Coach Steven, who was always there for moral support. I was never sure what he did as a coach. Coach Moore was the head track and field and football coach; he was dedicated and made sure all the athletes were taken care of. Several times, he drove me home from practices. Later in his career, for all the energy and time he put into his athletes, the high school named the track and field stadium after him.

Finally, there were two coaches, Coach Lo and Coach Timothy, who worked with me to perfect my three main running events, the 400-meter dash, the 200-meter dash, and the 800-meter dash. They played a huge role in making me as successful as I was. They never stopped believing in me, and they were dedicated to making me a great athlete. They treated me as a father would treat his child and made me feel safe and protected.

One time, Coach Timothy rushed to my house late at night when he heard things weren't the best there. I was more than just his athlete, and I wasn't the only athlete my coaches treated the same way they treated their own children.

No one in my family took as much interest in my success as my coaches did. I was content with the family I had created with my coaches and those on my track and field team. We were in one another's lives on and off the track. It was a family I had never imagined I would be a part of. That's how it had to be in order for us all to get through the season. We needed one another. That was the meaning of team that we had created, and I carried that definition to my college track and field team, hoping we would uplift one another and become successful Division I athletes.

CHAPTER 20

God's Hands on Me

My high school track and field days were over; my college track and field days were overflowing with things to do every day to challenge my running capabilities. The first year in college, I complained every day I walked on the track. It was just so hard, and I didn't understand that this was what it would take for me to get faster and better in my events. I despised every workout my coach gave us including weight training and bouncing my joints on what felt like sinking sand.

Every week was the same schedule—Monday, Wednesday, and Friday, weights at 10:00 a.m., and running practice at 7:00 a.m. or 2:00 p.m. every day depending on my event coach. Sometimes, we had practices three times a day in shorter times to meet the NCAA Division I training requirements for athletes.

I was also being challenged by my classes one assignment after another. Student athletes were required to check in with their academic advisors as well as their athletic advisors. It was a lot to juggle along with a job I had taken to help with my expenses. It was hard but manageable because I made sure the Lord was fully involved in my life.

I attended several Christian organizations on campus; I worshiped and met many students from all over the world. It was a life-changing experience. I went to Bible study every week with a few athletes; that was where I met some people who became lifelong friends, my family. God was the center of my life during my time there. He was the only father I knew, and I wanted to make him proud of me. I never asked myself who my biological father was thinking I would eventually find out.

A phone call changed my life.

"I think I found your father."

"Who's this?" I asked stunned.

"Your cousin. I think I've found him. His name is Gary, and he lives in Tennessee."

I was still in shock. He gave me Gary's phone number.

"Okay ... Thanks."

I stared at the numbers I had written down. Questions I had had would soon be answered. It did not help that his name was not on my birth certificate, but I was a step closer to knowing who my father was.

I anxiously dialed digit after digit. As I came to the last one, I closed my eyes, spoke to my heavenly father, and pressed dial. A part of me didn't want him to answer, but he did.

"Hello."

Unsure of what to say, I just spit it out: "Hey. Umm, my name is Grace, and I'm your daughter."

"Yes, your cousin said you would call me sometime. I wasn't sure when."

The door to a new beginning had opened, but I wasn't sure I should walk through it.

Years passed, and we talked frequently. I finally asked if he would be willing to get a DNA test. Everything in my life was unclear; I wanted to know just one thing for sure. I wanted to know if it was his blood running through my body.

"Grace, I know you're my daughter. We don't need a DNA test."

I was shocked by his lack of consideration for my feelings. My heart closed that moment to the idea that he was my father. If he was not willing to get a DNA test to prove the truth, I was unwilling to continue something that may not have been what it appeared to be. I needed clarity, and he deprived me of that again. I was not in the business of waiting for anyone to break my heart.

CHAPTER 21

The Glory Year

A wise person once told me that time flew by in college and that I was to enjoy every moment. That person was right. Three years had flown by; it was 2013, and I had only one year before I'd graduate. I wasn't sure what I would be doing after that. It didn't help that for the previous two years, I was turning in slow times on the track and wasn't improving.

As the year began, my coach sat me down and said that I was putting in the work in practices but that when it came to performing, it looked as though I were coasting. I pondered the reason for that and what could possibly be holding me back, and I concluded that it was my lack of trust in God and the buried voices of violent guardians or parents I had once confided in. My past was haunting me again and subconsciously. I'd been unaware of that. I wasn't being an asset to the team because I was still a slave to someone I thought was completely out of my life.

"Grace, what are your goals for this year?" she asked.

"To trust in God to lead my legs and take me further than ever."

She looked at me in awe, and being a believer herself, she didn't shut down the idea.

"Okay, that's good. Now what running time goals do you have?"

I knew she was asking for specifics. "I'd like to bring my four-hundred-meter time down to at least fifty-five seconds."

She looked at me as vibrantly as ever. "Good. I'll see you tomorrow for practice. We're done here," she said in her perkiest voice. I didn't know exactly what she felt about my answers because she seemed to be always happy and joyous. I loved that about her aside from her amazing coaching capabilities.

Race after race, God led me to some great victories, but I couldn't have done that without my teammates and our constant pushing one another. We had a bond no one could break. We were all giving 150 percent in the weight room and on the track. Our confidence in one another kept us striving for perfection. Competition after competition, we gradually improved, and when it was finally time for the indoor conference, we felt more than ready.

One time, we pulled up in our bus to our hotel for a meet, and our head coach stood and said, "All right, let's all stay focused. You know what to do, so take care of business, get some rest, and get ready to compete." He wasn't the best speech giver, but his facts were always right. It was time to take care of business, but more than anything, it was very important that I stayed steadfast in my faith in God. I was on a mission for my team but also for God to show everyone the blessings he had given me.

That night, I prayed to God for peace and a calm spirit for the next day. I closed my eyes and felt that my teammate and I were already preparing ourselves for our individual events, the 400-meter and the 200 meter. The 400 meter is considered one of the hardest races, but it was my race.

When my teammate and I arrived at the track, everyone was warming up. I had an hour before my first race, so I waited thirty minutes before I started warming up so I'd be ready just before the race and not psych myself out and start thinking I couldn't do it.

I asked the Lord to lead me to victory. I stepped on the track and approached the blocks, I spoke to God as my guide gracefully prepared the blocks. I positioned myself as perfect as perfect could get, took a deep breath, and waited for the gun to go off.

"On your mark …" *Pow!* We were off. God led my feet one step after another giving me the confidence I had never had before to run this race and gain a personal victory. It was the best individual race I had run all year, which earned my team at least two more points than I had ever been able to give them before. I placed sixth walking away with a copper medal but feeling that I was walking away with so much more.

The show wasn't over. I might not have made it to the finals in the 200 meter, but it was the last dash of the day. As a whole, my team was in fourth place with a chance to gain third depending on how we did in the 4 x 4 relay; four athletes on the same team were to run four hundred meters each and pass off the baton.

My Jamaican teammate and great friend Merissa Terkin was running first, and I was running last. She had the hardest part in the relay—Her responsibility was to start us off strong, though all the runners' performances were critical. Merissa began to cry not believing she would be able to complete her task. I took her hands and began to pray; with God, all things are possible, and he gave me strength. I knew she could do it and show the world that she had what it took.

We were running in the sixth lane, the hardest lane to compete in. Merissa stepped out on the track and prepared her blocks with the baton in her left hand. *Pow!* She started moving and was giving it all she had in spite of being discouraged. Before we knew it, she was on her last turn and in third position out of eight teams. She passed the baton to our second runner, who pushed us closer to second place. She passed the baton to our third runner, who got us even closer to second place by the time she passed the baton to me. My teammates had done well, but that wouldn't matter if I fell behind. I had a choice—to let fear get in the way of our victory or put myself in God's hands. I had to finish the race for myself, for my team, and for God, my father.

Brimming with confidence, I held out my hand in back of me, took the baton, and followed the footsteps of a woman on another team who was in the lead for three hundred meters. As I came around the corner approaching my last hundred meters, I shifted into a higher gear, and we won our heat.

Our conference hadn't believed in us because not only did we have a tough lane to compete in, but we had also been placed in the slow heat versus the fast heat that would guarantee us first, second, or at least third. We won our heat and put on one heck of a performance having given our all, but we had to wait for the fastest heat of the two to go in order to find out where we stood.

Pow! They were off, and the times were looking fast. We waited for the total result between the two heats. The times showed up on the screen. Our team had been second in our slow heat in a very challenging lane, and we had placed second overall by just seconds. To put the cherry on top, we had shattered our university record killing two birds with one stone.

As we stood on the podium and accepted our well-deserved medals, I thought about that indoor season, the best season I had running at my university. We got on the bus and headed to campus after three days of competition; we were all tired.

The next day, Coach called us to a meeting on the stadium stairs. There was something different about her look; it was as though she was about to give us some discouraging news. I was troubled. It wasn't going to be one of our typical meetings. Glory lasted only for a moment, and I was thinking that my joy would last only for a moment as well.

"Guys," she said, "I'll no longer be coaching you after outdoor season. I'm moving to Kentucky because my husband landed a job with an NFL team there. I wanted you guys to hear it from me before it got around as a rumor."

Shaking my head in disbelief, I became angry. I was speechless. I felt once again abandoned.

CHAPTER 22

Senior Year

Watch and pray so that you will not fall into temptation. The spirit is willing, but the flesh is weak.

—Matthew 26:41

Coach was gone. Again, I felt I had lost everything. My trust in God was being tested. When she left, she took a part of me along. Life seemed to have no purpose. I started just going through the motions to complete my senior year.

Constantly running through my mind was how meaningless the world was as Solomon had spoken about in Ecclesiastes. I started having dreams about not existing. Depression and I met again, but that time, it was more intense. I felt that I had died from the inside out. Depression was a toxic disease building up in me leaving a very bitter taste on my tongue. Because of all my discomfort, I imagined a world without me.

Due to all the people who sincerely cared about me, I was placed on antidepressants. KC in particular took on more than

I would have wanted anyone to. We were two peas in a pod. We were always together, and we loved ministering to others together. She wanted so desperately to help me, and I wanted so desperately for her to experience God's grace. KC and I were inseparable; we learned more and more about each other every day. We were devoted to each other and figured out suppressed things in ourselves that might separate us.

As I learned more about myself, I began experiencing a sense of suffocation that caused me to appear selfish. I was in shock as I began to unravel the darkness in my past, and I leaned on KC to help me get through the shock that I was experiencing because of traumatic things I finally allowed myself to remember.

KC was a writer, and so was I, so one day, KC came up with something we could do together that would release the bondage past experiences had us in: "We could write a poem together," KC exclaimed. "You might feel better just getting it out."

I looked at her as dead as someone in a grave. "Yeah, maybe … Okay."

I worked on the poem fervently and tried to be as honest and as creative as possible. Weeks later, I had finished it, and she found us a place where we could recite it. She invited several of our friends to come.

Prior to that, I had sought help from a counselor at the university. Years before that, I had seen a counselor; that hadn't worked out due to personal reasons, but that was not the case with the university counselor; he was one of the best. The first day with him, I sat in his office in silence, and that occurred during other sessions I had with him, but he never pushed me to speak about anything. One day, I said, "I think I'm upset about all the things that happened to me in the past. If I write down the lies and replace them with truths, perhaps I can begin to heal from them."

"That sounds like a great idea, Grace," he responded.

"I had thoughts about harming myself, but I don't want to die. That's why I'm here."

"It's good that you can identify truth through everything," he said.

"KC, my best friend, and I will write a poem together and perform it as a way to be free from all the things that oppress me. I love God so much that I want to be free of this desire to give up, so I have to try,"

I left my counselor's office that day feeling a tad relieved. I had spent a lot of time pondering the past and panicking over the future that would never come to be at the rate I was going.

"Grace, are you ready?" KC asked. "It's our chance to go up."

"Yes, I'm ready," I said though I was nervous.

She and I walked on stage. She appeared a little uncomfortable, and I was shaking and sweating. My heart was beating out of my chest, and my mind was all over the place. I had never been so scared in my life. I was about to reveal very sensitive parts of my life to what seemed like the world. I started off first with my portion of it.

I need a savior.

A plead of needing someone in my life, since my mother grabbed a knife and stabbed me, hindered me severely, here. In my heart. In which I hold dearly.

I was once a part of you whom I called mother,

Settled so graceful in the pit of your stomach oblivious to what the world had in store, and then you introduced me, loved me for only a second, closed your eyes, and let me go as I was sucked up into a tornado.

It's like the weather never clears, and like the tapping of a tree branch against a window in the midst of a storm, constantly I have fears,

Knowing for you the idea is no more.

Selfishly, all I wanted was just to be loved, blinded to truth people distorted my desire, reared me into the mire like the serpent in the story of Adam and Eve, and I was inevitably deceived.

I was young, as unclean became a part of me, snakes, serpents all
around, whispering in my ear an awful sound, "Come play
with me. Come sit on my lap. Come. I'll give you treats."
I found myself in this battle just desperately wanting to retreat.
Before the commander holds up his left hand with a gun, telling
me to take charge,
I am down in my blocks preparing for the next race to start.
I look to the left of me at my competition—she's vicious, quite
mysterious I look closer,
My heart began to pound at the sound of a voice that I buried
six feet under,
In a grave I visit every day,
A death of a woman who digs deeper and deeper, as I stand
among my contemptuous keeper.
It was like death, and the beginning of another war,
Her voice was like the sound of thunder in the midst of a storm,
Her appearance bared the shadow of a fierce beast, whom feasted
on my sorrow constantly.
Her touch was like lightning, sending electric shock throughout
my skin,
I thought my life might end, so I prayed,
Pleading to the Lord that I might stay, at first.
Then, my mind tug of war; is this a blessing or a curse?
See, I love the Lord wholeheartedly, but the grave that I visited
daily was actually mine. My mind was twisted like vines,
and I just wanted to recline to heaven with God.
I wanted the nerves in my head, the blood running through my
veins, the beating of my heart, and the air in my lungs to
subside,
For I wanted to die, but truthfully speaking, hidden beneath the
tears in my eyes, I was hungry for life,
Starving.
Starving. Angry. Surrounded by so many tangible human beings
and yet feeling invincibility.

Starving. Stuck in a battle within my mind disconnecting every part of me from true life.

Starving. Craving to be filled with the bread of life—the only thing that compensates and completely fills in the holes of strife.

The living Word, Jesus Christ, fills me up where food lacks.

The gaping pit in my heart, once the Grand Canyon, now starts to retract.

A gentle touch on my soul, from hands—strong enough to bear the weight of the world ... strong enough to bear the weight of the world while nailed down to a cross ... are now holding me.

Break this in remembrance of me, said thee.

He set off on a journey to set us free.

His vulnerable body, stark naked as on the day He was born.

But even further and deeper as He was beaten and ripped to His core.

He bore no shoes on his feet,

As the rocks embedded deeper and as his stomach wept,

Your first words might be defeat.

But see, spit upon facing brutality Jesus exclaimed, "Father, forgive them."

Completely unclothed and worn bearing no chains,

He could not resist his passionate love informing that "We're always welcomed in" despite sin.

He walks,

And while we stumble on our own faults, there's no tremble in his voice, for he made his choice, and so have I,

He's now "my" core. If you stripped me down, ripped me open inside, you would see him shining brighter as each day passes when I let him in.

Beneath my skin, I too bear the scars from before,

The shame from them I feel no more:

A heart once torn sown together reflected by Christ desire to mend my plead to cease the grief that seems as though it will never end.

We put no stumbling block in anyone's path, so that our ministry will not be discredited. Rather, as servants of God we commend ourselves in every way: in great endurance; in troubles, hardships and distresses; in beatings, imprisonments and riots; in hard work, sleepless nights and hunger; in purity, understanding, patience and kindness; in the Holy Spirit and in sincere love; in truthful speech and in the power of God; with weapons of righteousness in the right hand and in the left; through glory and dishonor, bad report and good report; genuine, yet regarded as impostors; known, yet regarded as unknown; dying, and yet we live on; beaten, and yet not killed; sorrowful, yet always rejoicing; poor, yet making many rich; having nothing, and yet possessing everything.

(2 Corinthians 6:3–10)

Could I believe I had everything with God, or would the things I felt I had lost continue to weigh me down as well as those around me? I wish I could say that after that day, things got better for me and that KC and I continued on a journey together with God as our rock, but something deep in me would not let me go, and I remained captive.

Months passed as we continued to confide too much in each other; eventually, it ripped us apart. I wanted a mother so badly that I tried to create her through KC, but she couldn't be my mother, and I couldn't be her friend. Everything became all about me, about helping me figure out a way to control the one thing consuming me—depression.

A big mistake we made was moving in with each other. Every day, we were flooded by our emotions that drained away and left us feeling spiritually depleted. I knew where I was spiritually because I had been there before, but KC was experiencing that for the first time. If I wouldn't talk to her, she felt she had done something wrong that made me hate her. Her worth was being dimmed daily, and I was responsible for that thought I didn't mean to have. I fell back into old habits and pushed her as far away as possible, and that led to our friendship being put on hold for what seemed like centuries.

We moved out of our apartment and stopped communicating. I never gave up on KC. I believe she gave up on me. I know it's selfish of me to think that considering what I had put her through, but as hard as she tried to keep our friendship and my life going, I was surprised at how easily she let me go. My world was shattered, and everyone around me saw that. I gave up on myself, but everyone who loved me kept fighting, which lit a spark in me. I started crawling, then walking, and then running again.

I thought about what I would do after I graduated, which was just around the corner. *Where will my degree take me? What are my career goals? Will I be able to get a job right away?* I had many such questions and no answers, and that made me anxious about my future. I wasn't sure what I wanted to do; I took time to think about that. I had always wanted to help people. Working in a hospital was definitely a plus. I loved God, so I figured I could plan my future around that notion. After much consideration and hair-pulling, I decided to become a physician assistant missionary so I could use medicine to cure physical pain and the Word of God to cure spiritual pain; I wanted to heal people's spirits.

I wanted to focus on what I thought God's plan for me was—to live my testimony to bring people comfort and healing. I looked online for summer missionary internships and found Step Out Ministries, a nonprofit that attracted college grads to the ministry. My heart was lit up with excitement when I applied for an internship there. As odd as this sounds, I really wasn't expecting to hear back from the organization, but two days later, I got a call.

"Hello," I said unsure of who was on the other end.

"This is the director of Step Out Ministries. We'd like to schedule you for an interview. Do you have time for an interview now?"

That caught me off guard, but I said, "Yes sir, most definitely," though I had only fifteen minutes to get to my next class.

"So tell me why you want to work with this organization."

"Well, I've always wanted to be a missionary, and I believe this is a step in the right direction to fulfilling that dream."

The interview went on, and I gave him sincere answers.

"Thanks so much for your time, Grace. We'll call you within the next three days with whether we feel you're a great fit for one of the mission sites."

"Yes sir. Thanks for the chance at a wonderful opportunity."

That call lifted my spirits. For once, I felt something was going to work out for me. Maybe I was destined to have some good luck. Getting ahead of myself as always, I began to prepare for what could be the opportunity of a lifetime. I prayed that the director would call back with good news.

Three days later, I was staring at my phone and sighing. I told God that if he wanted me to go, he would make everything work out. My phone started vibrating. I picked it up.

"Hello?"

"Is this Grace?"

"Yes it is."

"We'd like to offer you an internship."

I was overwhelmed with excitement. "Oh wow! Thanks so much!"

"But we want to offer you a position different from the one you applied for. We believe you'd be better suited as the MC."

The MC? I wondered. "I've never been an MC, but it sounds interesting. Sure, I'd love to."

"Great! We can't wait to meet you this summer."

I couldn't believe the opportunity God had just given me. As excited as I was, there was one thing about this internship that kept slipping my mind—I had to raise $1,500 for the training and a plane ticket to get there. The organization would provide me with food and housing. How was I going to raise $1,500 in just a few months? Only God was able to answer that question, and he miraculously did.

CHAPTER 23

God Never Ceases to Amaze

Summer was just around the corner, and I still had not raised the funds for my internship. My senior year was almost complete, and on top of that, KC and I had to move out of our apartment early due to mold infestation. I would be homeless until I started my internship. I decided to worry about my living situation when I got back from interning.

God does work in mysterious ways, and I got to experience his mysterious ways as he showed me that he could provide. He had actually been doing that for me all my life. Every Monday, Wednesday, and Friday, I went to a class on how to deal with grief. I hoped to learn how to deal with what I felt I had lost during my short life. This class was required for me to graduate, but I was also expecting to get something out of it for my emotional benefit.

My classmates were phenomenal, and my professor was much more than I had expected. For an assignment, we got into groups and discussed things we had been grieving. Noel was an outspoken girl in my group. If it hadn't been for her, what came next would never have happened.

One person after another shared his or her losses and referred to the books we had been reading in class. I was astonished that those in my group were willing to be so open, but I came to realize people just want to be heard and know that someone out there could actually care about their pain.

It came my turn to speak. I wanted to be heard. "I've lost everything from my mother to feeling that I exist, and I want to share that with world. God gave me this opportunity of a lifetime to intern as an MC. I have no idea how I'll raise the fifteen hundred dollars I need to do that, but I know I will. I pray that that's where God wants me to be, and I hope I can make a difference in someone's life by sharing mine because there's so much loss and brokenness in it but yet so much healing."

Noel said, "Why don't you sign up with GoFundMe? It's a site where people raise funds for their needs."

I looked at her in awe of the fact that she would even consider helping me and that everyone else in the group agreed with her. Yes, I could most definitely do that. I had never gotten much recognition as a child, and I never wanted much as an adult either. I wanted to be seen, but I never wanted to be in the spotlight.

The next day in class, my professor asked me, "Can I speak to you for just one second outside the room?"

"Sure," I said, and the two of us went into the hallway.

He said, "I was wondering if it would be okay if I pulled together a little gathering at my house for you to be able to go on your trip,"

Extremely surprised, I asked, "Like a fundraiser?"

"Yes. I want to open my home up for whatever you would like, and I'll require everyone in your class and some of my other classes to come and support you for a grade. Would you explain to the class a little bit of what you are trying to raise the money for?"

I was shocked. "Sure!"

We went back to class, and he said, "Good morning, class. Instead of writing a twenty-five-page paper as the final for this class, everyone is required to come support Grace at a fundraising event at my home. Grace will tell us all about what the fundraiser is for. Come on up, Grace."

I couldn't believe what was happening. I was nervous, but I stepped in the front of the class. "Hi, class. I've been given the opportunity to internship with a nonprofit Christian organization in Milwaukee, and I have to raise fifteen hundred dollars as well as enough money for the flight there. They offered me the MC position, and I'll be sharing God's testimony with others while engaging in projects that will help the community. I want to help others in their brokenness by sharing mine."

It was a gift to see all the faces expressing their willingness to help me. Noel helped me get the GoFundMe page up, and a day before the fundraising event at my professor's home, we were just $500 short. The day of the event, we were zero dollars short. I'd always loved writing and particularly poetry, so I decided to recite "Bondage," a poem I had written, at my professor's home.

Many showed up at the fundraiser, but KC was not among them. I loved her, but our friendship had been torn apart by my bitter, broken spirit. I wanted her to know that I was working on mending what was torn in my life and that this would be the start. I wanted her to know that for once I was trying to live. For months, she had been surrounded by my suicidal thoughts. It was stripping her of her life. I had let her down. I had killed her spirit. I couldn't blame her from stepping back from our friendship after so many long nights of me crying in her arms as pills lay on the floor of our apartment. The police took me to a hospital. KC had put her hands up and said in essence, "I have nothing more to offer you." I had to find something to live for, and I knew what I had to live without to do that. I had to quit seeking my mother in other women. I had to break that cycle.

That night, at my professor's house, I recited "Bondage."

In your womb I lay peacefully
Embracing the warmth within your body,

I'm tucked, like a child put to rest after a long day of what one
might call being innocent, I am buried beneath the layers
of your skin,

Comfortable I was until the day that I was conceived, and all
this came to an end,

I died. My mother had a miscarriage when she mistakenly
carried me and then pushed me out of her womb into a pit
of darkness with only a tad bit of light,

And it was this same tunnel, unbearable, fearful as I reach my
left and then right-hand darkness; it stripped away all my
sight,

I wept and I pleaded for something everyone seemed to not have,

And because of this even the simplest things could not make
me laugh.

How could I?

And a world such as this where I was repetitiously wondering
within a bliss,

How could I?

When everyone but I seemed to connect

While this bond I processed depicted an age far beyond my years
as it bereaved me of rest.

Twisting and turning within my sleep, I tugged away at what
seemed to take the appearance of a piece of string dragging
from me,

Thorns poking away at it as it trailed through the dirt that
grinded against its outside causing it to sting, rocks pierced
through it as it whispered in my ears,

I will never disappear,

I opened my eyes as wide as I could hoping that this was a
dream,

As sweat rushed to the outer potion of my body, my heart
expeditiously beating, head about to explode from all the
insufferable thoughts, with what little air I had left in me
I screamed,

What was this thing that clanged?

To everyone else it was invisible but to me it was as clear as crystal.

There were times when it took control,

But that was only when I got splinters within the grips of my hands and achingly had to let go.

More times than I would like, I was losing this battle of tug of war.

Then one day, I decided I could not take it anymore, I dropped the cord,

It swooped under my feet, dropped me to the ground face first, cuts embedded within my fragile skin,

Blood gushing out from underneath my pores, as it tugged and tugged and lured me in,

I thought the agony would never cease,

Please, I cried and cried.

Worn to a degree that numbed my body and torn in a way that posed the question why me?

It was as though I was drowning in the midst of my own sorrow tangled within this string, gasping for air with my head tilted up.

I think I'm going to hurl

Hesitantly I let out a shout.

Then without a doubt, cut went the string; and I distinctively heard a voice say, "Congratulations! It's a girl!"

Everyone clapped and cheered after I recited my poem. I was looking to the future. "I'm proud to announce that I have exceeded my goal! Thank you all so much for your help and support, and thank you, professor, for allowing me to use your home and believing in the next steps I am to take in my life."

I sighed, looked up at the sky, embraced God's blessings, and thanked him.

CHAPTER 24

An Unforgettable Summer

> When I discovered your words, I devoured them.
> They are my joy and my heart's delight, for I bear
> your name, O Lord God of Heaven's Armies.
> —Jeremiah 15:16 (NLT)

My church family came to watch me walk the stage at graduation and then to take me back to Daytona and spend a few days with them before my trip. Everything was working out for the best. Though nobody from my biological family attended the ceremony, my best friend and his mother came.

Even though it rained hard that day and I ended up with frizzy hair, a wet dress, and muddy heels, the day was perfect. I had graduated from college and was surrounded by my loved ones. I was sad to be leaving my running behind me, but I had run competitively for four years and was happy with what I had accomplished. What more could anyone ask for? I had wanted to find something to live for, and at that point in my life, I had found a million things to live for.

I took a deep breath when we drove off from college. In three days, I would head to Milwaukee for my internship. I was excited about that, but the antidepressants I was on made it hard for me to express my excitement. I never understood why doctors prescribed antidepressants; it seemed that they made me more depressed than happy. My moods would change, and it was hard for me to be motivated to do anything. I believed something was wrong with my medication.

When I arrived in Milwaukee, I put on my mask as I walked over to a group holding a sign that read, "Welcome Step Out Volunteers. You Made It!" With feelings of discomfort, I walked up to one of the women and said, "Hello. My name is Grace."

She said, "Hello. My name's Nya. Just go to that table over there and pick up your name tag and organizational package."

I somehow felt that my words from that point on would not be my own; I needed the Holy Spirit to get me through the unfamiliarity I was feeling. I checked in and went back to Nya and asked, "Nya where will you be working this summer?"

She said, "In Milwaukee. I'll be the team leader."

"I'll be the MC for that mission site. What a coincidence," I said.

From that point on, Nya and I were inseparable; we talked about ourselves and what had brought us to Step Out Ministries. It was comforting to have connected with someone who had decided to embark on a journey similar to mine.

Orientation took place in a hotel conference room, and I met the others who would be a part of our mission site. There was Blu, the music leader and lead singer, Nate and Gerry, who were the handymen in the group, the construction team duo, and Nya, the team leader, whose job was to keep everyone in the group mentally, physically, and emotionally stable so we could fulfill our mission work. I would be the MC, the voice of the group, the ministry, and God.

Unfortunately, the internal battle I was fighting burst out, and all at once, I was exposed, and it was weighing down my team. At the end of orientation, when the directors told me, "Grace, we're sending you home," I had nothing to say. I had known this was coming. I knew it was not fair to my team or the ministry for me to pose as something I was not—free. I was in captivity, and if they were not careful, my team would have been captive as well.

I knew they had made the right decision, but I felt defeated, and that made me angry. I pointed fingers at them and questioned their spirits and their association with God. However, they were set on sending me home. I was angry at the world and at God. I felt that because I didn't have parents or family who had my back, people and life would run over me as it appeared they were doing that moment. They knew I was on antidepressants; they knew I had given up everything to be there, but still, I was being released.

When I had gotten to Milwaukee, my emotions were all over the place. I was unable to pay attention, and I was saying things I would have never said otherwise. I spent all training week trying to balance my mood but could not. Something wasn't right. I didn't understand at first why the organization decided to do what they did, but looking back, I think it was for the good.

I cried. My broken heart ached. Once again, my life had been shattered, and I was unsure of what to do next. I had to let my church members know that I would be returning sooner than I had planned. The money I had raised went to cover bills, certain obligations to keep me on my feet. I had counted on being paid at the end of my internship as had been the plan.

I had gone to Milwaukee ready for an unforgettable, life-changing journey. I had been ready to break the chains that were preventing me from experiencing full surrender and complete freedom in Christ. The Bible reads,

> Come to me, all you who are weary and burdened, and I will give you rest. Take my yoke upon you and learn from me, for I am gentle and humble in heart, and you will find rest for your souls. For my yoke is easy and my burden is light.
>
> (Matthew 11:28–30)

I wanted to come to him, but everything in me just would not. I felt I was someone completely different from what God had intended me to be. I had been about to become the voice of a nonprofit Christian organization when I was not even sure who I was. I had no voice.

I walked away from Step Out Ministries feeling that my antidepressants rather than my relationship with Christ had identified me. Another door was shutting in my life. Tears filled my eyes and my spirit as I tried to figure out what lesson God was trying to teach me.

Luckily for me, one church family had a spare room I could stay in for the summer until I figured out what to do next. I got off the plane and cried in their arms. For weeks, I was overwhelmed with sorrow and stress. I was lost. I was spiritually starving. I got on my knees and prayed for answers.

That went on until I decided that everything happened for a reason. I got myself motivated to get a summer job. Things then began to fall into place. I went out dressed professionally and gave my resume to the managers of some fast-food restaurants, and I landed a job at burger place in Daytona. And on top of that, the Lord opened an opportunity for me to sing in the band at the church I'd been baptized in. Being a part of the band was something I'd always wanted to do. I realized that just when I had thought everything was going right according to my own desires, the Lord had shown me his desires for me; I had wanted to go to Milwaukee, but God wanted me in Dayton and to be closer to him. My plan for my life was not God's plan, so I embraced whatever was to come next, and I decided that I needed God, not antidepressants. I made a promise to get closer to God through prayer and reading of his Word every day.

I went to Lifeway, a well-known Christian bookstore, for something to guide me through the Bible. I came across a devotional, *Breaking Free*, by Beth Moore, and I instantly knew it was exactly what I needed. I was excited. I wish I could tell you that it motivated me to devote myself to spending more time with God, but waking up every day and spending time with God was challenging; I was tired. I had to force myself to spend time with God. I lacked desire. I felt that I was drowning and that God would have to dive in and bring me to the surface.

I slept. I worked. I woke. I read. I prayed. I ate. And then I repeated the cycle throughout the week aside from Sundays, when I sang at church minutes after getting off the night shift at my job. I was at the bottom of the ocean just waiting for that moment when I would get back up to the surface again. As the pills exited my body and God's true verses entered my veins, I slowly felt the weight leave me. My prayers began to be sincere, and I felt I was free.

> I have called you back from the ends of the earth, saying, "You are my servant." For I have chosen you and will not throw you away. Don't be afraid, for I am with you. Don't be discouraged, for I am your God. I will strengthen you and help you. I will hold you up with my victorious right hand.
>
> (Isaiah 4:9–10)

Before I knew it, the summer was over, the resentment I felt toward God was gone, and I knew that it was not God's fault. With the help of the amazing devotional, "Breaking Free," I broke free from the world's idea of healing and embraced God's idea of healing by stopping taking antidepressants and increasing my dosage of God's truth.

CHAPTER 25

Fifth-Year Graduate Student

It had finally become time for me to leave my home, but before I left, I spent close to a thousand dollars rescuing a dachshund named Angel. She was the sweetest dog, and it was a blessing to be able to take her home with me to be a part of my life.

I was content with the relationship I had built with Christ alone, so at the time, I did not want friends; I felt I didn't need them. Angel was all I desired, and I was going to love her like a child. Angel was the smartest dog I had ever had. Actually, she was the only dog I had ever had. She was cooperative and extremely loving.

When I arrived back in Gainesville, I had to find a place for Angel until I could come up with money for the pet fee my apartment complex required. I felt awful about the situation; Angel had been confused being moved from place to place. One of my friends, Naamah (beautiful, agreeable), from my college track and field team suggested that I talk to her sister. I had not met her sister, and Naamah and I had had disagreements about biblical truth and had constantly challenged each other on the topic.

I texted Naomi, Naamah's sister, that I needed a temporary place for Angel, and she agreed to take her in. I hurried over to her place with Angel, a crate, food, bowls, and some toys. I rang the doorbell, and Naomi answered the door. Someone said, "Hey Grace! Do you remember me?" I didn't, and I said so. "You don't remember Naomi and me running on the college cross-country team with you?"

"No, not really," I said. Many women had come and gone on the team. "But it is nice to see you or meet you again," I said.

Naomi asked, "Is Angel potty trained?"

I was unsure considering I had just gotten Angel, but I said yes. I told them just to cover myself, "If you have the time, you guys could walk her in the morning, or if y'all would like me to walk her, I'll come in the morning, afternoon, and evening to make sure she doesn't use the bathroom on your floor."

"That would be great considering we have very busy schedules and won't have much time to watch your dog," Naomi said.

I didn't have much time either, but Angel was ultimately my responsibility.

CHAPTER 26

Overwhelmed

It is for freedom that Christ has set us free. Stand
firm, then, and do not let yourselves be burdened
again by a yoke of slavery.

—Galatians 5:1

For once in my life, I felt overwhelmed with joy instead of pressure
or sorrow. I was what everyone hoped I would be. I was happy. I was
working in the kitchen at a well-known Christian camp and sharing
the gospel with college-aged Christians; I was hoping to make a
difference in their lives.

My approach to living and sharing the gospel of the Lord was
a little direct and stern. My strong personality caused me to forget
the enjoyment that comes with the life God had given me as I was
striving to accomplish God's purpose for me. I wanted to help people
acknowledge whatever was keeping them in captivity and inspire
them to overcome whatever stood in the way of their freedom.
Everyone has some sort of obstacle that has placed a hold on his or
her progression in life. If I didn't progress, I couldn't heal, and if I
remained oppressed, how could I help others to become free?

On the Fourth of July, the camp threw a huge celebration that included fireworks. It was such a beautiful night; I felt free of all the negatives in my past. The next morning, I made coffee for the kitchen manager and began to make breakfast. By the time my partner walked through the door, the girls and I were working on lunch; we were way ahead of schedule, so I logged on to my social media page to see what my friends were doing.

I had received a notification from one of my high school friends I had met through Jariel. As I read his message, my breath was taken away.

> Grace, one of our friends have been murdered, Gabriel, and I believe your brother Josiah was there in the home as well because they've identified two bodies but one has not been identified. It might be Josiah. Call him and make sure it was not Josiah. God, I pray he's okay.

I immediately called Josiah, but my call went to voice mail. I looked on Josiah's Facebook page to see if he had messaged Gabriel. "Who is down to do something for July 4th?" Gabriel had asked. Underneath Gabriel's comment was an icon that showed someone had replied several times to his question. I prayed to God that it was not Josiah. I just knew my brother could not be dead. I had just seen him before accepting the job at camp. I could still hear his voice and smell his scent as he held me insisting I would see him again. I knew God had heard my plea a year ago when I asked him to keep Josiah safe. He and I were working together to succeed, and we were doing well. I scrolled my cursor over the reply icon. Josiah had replied to Gabriel, "What's the plan?" That's as far as I read. Whatever the plan had been, they had been in it together.

I went numb. I was sure my brother was dead. I left the kitchen in tears; I wanted to talk with a women I had grown close to; my burden was too hard to bear alone. I met up with her and said, "My brother was murdered last night."

"I am so sorry, Grace." She lowered her head in sorrow. We shared my pain. I wondered why this had happened to such an amazing person who was striving to make something of his life. Why had God called him home in this particular moment in my life where I was finally feeling better? I was sad. My younger brother was dead.

CHAPTER 27

A Deep, Dark, Unwelcome Secret

No one lights a lamp and hides it in a clay jar or puts it under a bed. Instead, they put it on a stand, so that those who come in can see the light. For there is nothing hidden that will not be disclosed, and nothing concealed that will not be known or brought out into the open.

—Luke 8:16–17

My brother's death would either tear me down or give me the strength I'd need to persevere. I had always been determined to be strong no matter what life threw at me. Some days, I would drown in my sorrow, but other days, I would swim determined to get to the other side of that sorrow.

Josiah had had a great spirit. He was more than a brother. He was a bright light in a world of darkness. I regretted not being able to save him and return the favor he once did for me without knowing it. It was on a night that change my perspective on trust and men, African American men to be precise. That night, I had stared into the eyes of someone caught in the devil's grip.

Auntie Bella had taken a weekend trip to see her sisters, and she had left my brother and me in the house with her boyfriend. I went to my mother's room and knocked on the door; I needed some toilet paper. He answered the door, and my spirit felt that something was extremely wrong. Everything within me told me to turn away, but being the determined person I was, I asked him, "May I have some toilet paper?"

He grinned at me as if he was planning something. All the signs were there to run, but I ignored them. He got some toilet paper, but he dangled it in front of me. "Here it is," he said, so I walked over to him. He grabbed me and threw me to the floor. My mind was slow at processing what was about to happen, but as he pressed his entire body on mine, I realized what he was about to do. He craved me just as a hungry person craves food, and he was trying to devour me.

"Josiah!" I yelled at the top of my voice, and he immediately let me go. I got up and ran as fast as I could to Josiah's room.

"Hello," he said completely unaware of what had just happened. Feeling as though I would be protecting not only myself but everyone else, I went to my room and locked the door. I thanked God that Josiah had been there. That was not the first time an older man had been attracted to me. As I wrote earlier, my cousin had sexually preyed on me several times when I was seven until I was twelve. He would look at me. He would give me candy and smile at me. I would smile back because I was a very joyful girl. He would creep into my room at night, grab my tiny body, place me on top of him, and do things to me while I was sleeping. In my innocence, I believed him when he said it was just a game of hide and seek. He would lie on me or have me lie on him.

I finally realized there was something more to this simple game he claimed we were always playing when, at age nine, I told my youngest cousin that I had a crush on James, a friend of the family.

My older cousin heard that and proclaimed, "You are not to date anyone! You are way too young to date!"

That confused and frightened me. I felt he was attempting to control my every move so that he would not lose me as his women-girl. As the years passed, I began to cover up my body; I wore winter clothes in the summer. I was hot, but it was the only way I felt I had a small amount of control over the situation.

Why didn't I tell someone you ask? Because when my cousin played this game, I never screamed; I remained quiet out of fear and allowed my cousin to do whatever he desired. It made me feel so dirty, ashamed, and helpless. Somehow, however, I knew God loved me even if my cousin was toying with the true definition of love.

When my cousin started playing his game with other cousins, I took a step back and realized that this was incest. That was when I started running away and hoped to never look back. I fell to my knees and prayed to God for forgiveness. I felt I had committed an unforgiveable sin. I no longer wanted to be a part of such toxic behavior, and that was why the night my brother saved me, I found the courage to fight back, not just sit in silence.

Josiah had been the light in a very dark place. I was motivated to fight for life and truth. That was the problem, wasn't it? My brother had to go so that Christ could be my light and protector while my brother was just my brother. But the truth was that God had had nothing to do with my brother's death and neither had I. I had to accept the fact that he was dead and that God's only role was to comfort me.

> For the Lord will not cast off forever, but, though he cause grief, he will have compassion according to the abundance of his steadfast love.
>
> (Lamentations 3:31–32)

CHAPTER 28

Strength through a Weary Body

In the same way, the Spirit helps us in our weakness. We do not know what we ought to pray for, but the Spirit himself intercedes for us through wordless groans. And he who searches our hearts knows the mind of the Spirit, because the Spirit intercedes for God's people in accordance with the will of God. And we know that in all things God works for the good of those who love him, who have been called according to his purpose.

—Romans 8:26–28

A part of me died along with my brother. I was dying from the inside out. I could not eat or sleep. I was overwhelmed by the pain my brother's death was causing me. The entire camp was praying for me, so I knew my weakened body would regain strength; I was not in this alone.

One phone call after another from family and friends told me that we shared the pain. As I packed for my unexpected trip home, I heard a director outside my cabin say, "I thought you said your brother just got married."

"No. I said my brother was murdered. I'll be back in a week."

A coworker drove me to the airport. On the way, I looked out the window at the sky and said, "God, I'm ready." I was ready to face truth. I was ready to plan a beautiful ceremony for Josiah. He deserved that.

The Lord was with me throughout the beautiful ceremony; I was never alone. I was able to comfort others, and I felt that I was where God wanted me to be. My brother was gone. I tried to ignore that awful truth because that was how I dealt with pain. God gave me the strength I needed to get through the initial passing of my younger brother, and at the time, that was all I needed.

> Now Cain said to his brother Abel, "Let's go out to the field." While they were in the field, Cain attacked his brother Abel and killed him. Then the Lord said to Cain, "Where is your brother Abel?" "I don't know," he replied. "Am I my brother's keeper?"
> (Genesis 4:8–9)

It was finally time for us to all say goodbye to Josiah. Family and friends stood together in his presence one last time. Time kept moving, but life was frozen, and my heart stopped beating along with his for a moment. As I realized his spirit had detached from his body when the bullet went through his young head, a part of me left too. I asked myself if I had failed at being my brother's keeper.

I had invited Auntie Bella to the service, but she was late. I remembered asking Josiah one time if Auntie Bella would ever be our mother. He looked me in the eye and said, "That woman will never be our mother. Stop dreaming and wishing she would because she never will be."

Auntie Bella rushed into the church shoving her way to the front of the lineup and drawing attention to herself as she always did. The funeral home director asked me, "Would you like me to escort her out of here?"

"No," I said. "It's all right."

My auntie was crying dramatically, my sister was weeping, and my older brother was speechless. I was preparing to stand up and speak when a poem my brother had written started going through my mind. I had found it on his Facebook page. My brother had been blessed with so many talents; he could write, he was a genius and very good at math, and he was honest, one of his qualities that I had been sure would land him a wonderful wife one day. No matter how many times life knocked him down, he always got right back up. It never dawned on me that he would think otherwise until I read his poem.

> I feel I was born to lose,
> So I'll die to win,
>
> Even when my backs to the ground,
> And life has me pinned,
>
> I'll look it in the eye,
> With an arrogant grin,
> And exclaim,
> I will not bow,
>
> I will not break,
> I'll figure out a way,
> To shut this world away,
> I will not fall,
> I will not faint,
> This unconquerable spirit you'll never taint,
>
> If giving in is the right thing to do,
> I'll die a fool,

I'll see this battle through,
In the heat of the moment,
I refuse to lose,
Even if I have to keep it cool,
I will not bow,
I will not break,
I refuse to fall,

And lose it all,

I'll start to crawl,
Because,
I was born to lose,
So I'll die to win,

Making failure my foe,
And success my friend,
I will not bow.

He had fought a battle that he felt he had not lost. Despite what the world told him about what he had been born to be, he refused to admit defeat. He was no loser. That is why I believe he made the right choice before he took his last breath; that was to follow God, because that was the only way he would truly win. As far as I knew, my brother had died an unbeliever, and I did not know if I would ever see him again.

Someone once told me that when I got the opportunity to speak to a crowd, I should make sure to leave an impactful message that would awaken their souls. I walked up without an ounce of anxiety in my body; that was because part of me was numb. However, there was hope. Even though I missed my brother dearly, I loved and trusted in God, and I wanted people to see through their grief.

He loves us more than air itself to cease His breath and die to self;
I'd say I love Him more than air itself;
The desire I feel for Him cannot be replaced, while people
ponder over the riches of this world deceitfully believing in
its temporary comfort, He is my wealth;
His gentle touch seeping to my heart from my skin, waiting to
get in.

I began to sing as a part of the poem I wrote.

For He loves us, oh how He loves us oh how He loves, He is
Jealous for me loves like a hurricane and I am a tree bending
beneath the weight of His wind and mercy.
Despite the bitter seasoning marinating as sin, as my pores open
it gets in and in;
He whispers, soft-spoken, sincerely to me;
His passion and His strongest desire is to keep me set free, Not,
not acknowledging my wants but sternly giving me exactly
what I need;
Graciously, He wants nothing in return;
His only yearn is that I except the flowers presented to me daily
because He believes that I am worthy;
Me, living in sin can and has caused me to be dirty;
To love and be in love, requires patience;
He waits silently right beside my bedside hoping for life over death;
Caressing my hands proclaiming to me that He has never left,
and never will;
He says the key to trusting and believing in this, in me, is Psalm
46:10, "to be still and know that I am God!"

I knew that God was God and that that was all that mattered.
I walked away filled with hope instilled by Christ that I would be
resilient even in my despair. I was ready for the next steps in my life
with God at the center of it.

CHAPTER 29

Boot Camp Part I

Relationships are difficult, and that's especially true with the ones you dedicate a lifetime to staying committed to. Imagine the start of a 5k race, 3.1 miles of pure agony. The race begins, and you are regretting that you had entered it. Halfway through, you begin to look down instead of looking forward and ask, "Where's the end?"

Who would have thought that at age twenty-three, I would be burying my younger brother? Who would have thought that at age twenty-three, I would have lost so much but also gained so much through Christ? I felt that sadness had become my sin and that I was walking through life aimlessly and seemingly alone. Where was the God with whom I had begun a relationship ten or twelve years earlier?

I had not always felt alone. At some point, there was this someone, this girl, this woman who decided to be a part of my life despite my wanting to be alone. She basically took on my dreadful problems and became a part of the greatest roller coaster ever. I grew to love her, but the bumps became too much to handle. We were young adults trying to figure out how to live, but the mistake we made was deciding to be there for each other.

Despite my doubts, our friendship developed into a sisterhood, and that is when I knew that she would never stop loving me as one of hers. However, we attacked each other to the point that we were nothing like ourselves. I was still grieving my brother's death. I did not really want to be angry at God and think that he had taken my brother, so I took it out on everything else in my life including my sister and dearest friend.

I was heading to army boot camp in hopes of coming out a soldier. I cannot remember what went on during that time because while my physical body was in boot camp, my mind mourned the loss of my brother and the uproar I had caused back home. I could not focus; it felt good to be away from everyone so that I might be able to redirect my attention.

The first day of boot camp was simple. They took our belongings and threw some of them on the ground. We stood in a line while we waited on our bay assignments. A bay was a room that sixty-eight females shared. It had one big bathroom that had one big shower. I could not believe that. I had a phobia about being naked in front of others; I called it nakaphobia. If my recruiter had told me about the shower situation, I don't think I would have enlisted. Others in my bay told me I'd get used to it, but I didn't think so. It was not my fault that I felt that way; it was my predator's fault. Children who are molested have more uncomfortable moments than they have comfortable moments. I did not like wearing clothes that were tight because I did not want to attract the dark face that had sought to extinguish God's light in me.

God has shown me things throughout my journey that allowed me to keep going and recognize the speed bumps. The Lord gives me just the right tools so that I slow down just enough to maintain mobility and keep going. That's the key to seeing what God wants us to see our lives as and not as the world does.

However, I was willing to adjust considering it would be nice to disappear from the turmoil I had left back home. I wanted to run away from the idea that I had lost my brother. So I decided that I was going to go through boot camp as though it were a fantasy because that is exactly what it felt like until God showed up and showed me differently.

The morning of our second day of boot camp, angry people in what we called uniforms woke us up rudely and told us to go line up outside. It was the first time I had heard of being in formation, that is, with enough space between us so that officers could walk among us. I learned to stand at attention with heels together, feet pointing out at 45-degree angles, and legs straight but without locking the knees.

The chest is lifted, the back is arched, and shoulders are square and even. Arms hang straight down alongside the body without stiffness, and the wrists are straight with the forearms. Hands are cupped but not clenched with palms facing the legs. The head is erect and held straight to the front with the chin drawn in slightly so that the axis of the head and neck is vertical. Eyes are to the front with the line of sight parallel to the ground. The weight of the body rests equally on the heels and balls of the feet, and silence and immobility are required.

Yes, I know that's very specific and technical, but as I got used to it, I realized it was more than just a command; it was a way of defining my safe space. The numbness I felt in my body during this stationary drill matched the numbness I felt inside. Every time the sergeant called us to attention, I felt I could maintain that position for days. I felt that nothing could touch me, and that even if anything did, I would bleed just enough that I would not die. I was so close but yet so far away. I was shallow but not defeated. I was numb but still alive. I was breathing though at times I felt that there was no air.

My soul was in a dilemma split between two distinct feelings. My soul was full of pain because I missed my brother, but at times, it was filled with hope because I would not allow myself to be angry with God. I loved God but felt distant from him. Those command words became my safe place: "Group attention!" I never really paid much attention at boot camp; I went through the motions. I did, however, want to succeed; my siblings and I never quit.

After orientation and processing, our training began. Our sergeants prepared us for the brutality we would experience. I was living in a blur I followed suit not knowing what to expect but not caring about it.

> Endure suffering along with me, as a good soldier of Christ Jesus. Soldiers don't get tied up in the affairs of civilian life, for then they cannot please the officer who enlisted them. And athletes cannot win the prize unless they follow the rules. And hardworking farmers should be the first to enjoy the fruit of their labor. Think about what I am saying. The Lord will help you understand all these things.
>
> Always remember that Jesus Christ, a descendant of King David, was raised from the dead. This is the Good News I preach. And because I preach this Good News, I am suffering and have been chained like a criminal. But the word of God cannot be chained. So I am willing to endure anything if it will bring salvation and eternal glory in Christ Jesus to those God has chosen.
>
> This is a trustworthy saying. If we die with him, we will also live with him. If we endure hardship, we will reign with him. If we deny him, he will deny us. If we are unfaithful, he remains faithful, for he cannot deny who he is. (2 Timothy 2: 3–13)

I knew what the Lord desired of us as soldiers for him, which in turn would lead me to victory in uniform.

"SPC Still!"

"Yes Sergeant."

"You're going to be bay leader since you're the oldest."

"Yes Sergeant," I said as if I had a choice in the matter.

I had no idea what it meant to be a bay leader, but I would do the best I could not just for me but for the others in my bay. I learned I would have to make sure that the bay was always clean and that everyone's bed was made correctly with what was called a hospital corner with flat sheets (no fitted sheets here) tucked under the mattress and the corners folded at 45 degree angles and tight as a drum. If a quarter dropped on the bed bounced, we had it made. If it didn't, we'd hear about it from our sergeants. I decided to never unmake my bed; I would sleep on top of the blanket and sheets.

As bay leader, I had to delegate females to be fire guards when others were sleeping. Being fire guard was no fun when you wanted to be asleep; it's more of an exercise in discipline than anything else, but when I was on fire guard, I would take showers alone because of my discomfort. I had gained the others' respect somehow, so they allowed me that privilege.

I had to handle disagreements between the other PFCs; I did my best to assist everyone, and one way I did that was to have meetings. It felt like I was having meetings daily about one thing or another. It got to the point that some females were beginning to feel that the meetings were ineffective.

One time, one female felt I had taken the side of another female over her in a dispute, but I cared about them both and I felt their dilemma was due to immature behavior. I wanted them to see their goal—to become soldiers. I was disappointed that they were allowing something so small to affect a huge part of their lives. I can't make others change their ways; I can only pray that they choose the right course of action. I have always been grateful to God for allowing me to look past trivial things and stay focused on the big picture.

I began to develop feelings for those in my bay, and I wanted them all to become soldiers with me just as when I get to heaven, I want to see many others there with me. While most of them did make it through in-processing, some didn't, and that made me feel I had failed them. It reminded me of the parable of the lost sheep.

> What do you think? If a man owns a hundred sheep, and one of them wanders away, will he not leave the ninety-nine on the hills and go to look for the one that wandered off? And if he finds it, truly I tell you, he is happier about that one sheep than about the ninety-nine that did not wander off. In the same way your Father in heaven is not willing that any of these little ones should perish.
> (Matthew 18:12–14)

CHAPTER 30

Boot Camp Part II

"May God be with us all on this journey to becoming soldiers, and may his will be done," I prayed while marching to our company, I knew the Lord would hear me and help me. When we got to our company, we were sectioned off into platoons by last names. God had spared me because I was one letter away from being a part of the platoon that had a drill sergeant who constantly yelled. We called her the witch. For whatever reason, female drill sergeants were the worst. It was as if they were trying to prove themselves to the male drill sergeants and show them that they were strong enough to wear the uniform.

Her name was Drill Sergeant E, and her counterpart was Drill Sergeant Lang, and he just fed her fury. I had never met two drill sergeants who could scare me senseless the way they did. But here is the thing—drill sergeants are symbols of excellence at boot camp; they are expert at all warrior tasks and battle drills, they live army values, exemplify the warrior ethos, and most important, they are the epitome of the army as a profession.

Drill sergeants are responsible for coaching, counseling, and mentoring hundreds if not thousands of civilians who want to become soldiers. Drill sergeants are with their privates from before dawn until lights out. Soldiers emulate everything they do. Being a drill sergeant is one of the most demanding and difficult jobs in our army, but it is one of the most rewarding. What drill sergeants do for soldiers will affect their entire military lives.

I had not been granted the luxury of having Drill Sergeant E and Drill Sergeant Lang as my drill sergeants; I had Drill Sergeant Waldo and Drill Sergeant Ritz, who were quite different from the other drill sergeants. They treated us like adults and would reason with us rather than humiliate us.

The way I felt inside did not match the way I felt outside; I wanted to feel pain all over. I wanted them to punish me so that my body would ache as much as my heart was aching. I wanted to taste how it would feel to be near death because emotionally, I wanted to be with my brother. My sergeants' approach, however, was gentle; they reasoned with us as good people hoping to make us good soldiers. Instead of instilling fear in us, they instilled wisdom in us. However, I was screaming for a harsh punishment. We had become the ate-up platoon, and most of the soldiers in our platoon saw our sergeants' kind and gentle gestures as a weakness, and they tried to run over the sergeants. Their kindness had become our weakness, and it was embarrassing. I wanted to just listen and behave, but not everyone in the platoon had that mindset. I felt that my sergeants' wisdom would take me far as a soldier.

One fellow soldier truly inspired me to press on through my pain caused by the physical training we went through. Vera gave it all she had. She passed on to me her desire to excel in doing push-ups. Every night, she would get on the floor and practice push-ups. When she first started, she could not do one, not correctly at least. She could not even lift herself up. But she worked at it, and she was an inspiration to me. She had accepted Jesus as her savior; God was her inspiration to succeed.

Every soldier had to pass the Army Physical Fitness Test (APFT) before being deemed a soldier. The APFT consisted of two minutes of push-ups, two minutes of sit-ups, and a two-mile run. Vera never gave up. Every night, she did more and more push-ups, and I knew she would pass the APFT. Her determination rubbed off on me; I promised myself that I would help as many of those girls succeed at being a soldier. I was on a mission that would allow me to not focus on my personal struggles but rather to focus on others. She helped me realize that there was more to life than my personal problems. Isn't that what God does for us as well? He tells us that we have strength in him if we believe that anything is possible. It reminded me of one of my favorite parables when Jesus healed a demon-possessed boy in Mark 9:14–27.

> When they returned to the other disciples, they saw a large crowd surrounding them, and some teachers of religious law were arguing with them. When the crowd saw Jesus, they were overwhelmed with awe, and they ran to greet him. "What is all this arguing about?" Jesus asked. One of the men in the crowd spoke up and said, "Teacher, I brought my son so you could heal him. He is possessed by an evil spirit that won't let him talk. And whenever this spirit seizes him, it throws him violently to the ground. Then he foams at the mouth and grinds his teeth and becomes rigid. So I asked your disciples to cast out the evil spirit, but they couldn't do it." Jesus said to them, "You faithless people! How long must I be with you? How long must I put up with you? Bring the boy to me." So they brought the boy. But when the evil spirit saw Jesus, it threw the child into a violent convulsion, and he fell to the ground, writhing and foaming at the mouth. "How long has this been happening?" Jesus asked the boy's father.

He replied, "Since he was a little boy. The spirit often throws him into the fire or into water, trying to kill him. Have mercy on us and help us, if you can." "What do you mean, 'If I can'?" Jesus asked. "Anything is possible if a person believes." The father instantly cried out, "I do believe, but help me overcome my unbelief!" When Jesus saw that the crowd of onlookers was growing, he rebuked the evil spirit. "Listen, you spirit that makes this boy unable to hear and speak," he said. "I command you to come out of this child and never enter him again!" Then the spirit screamed and threw the boy into another violent convulsion and left him. The boy appeared to be dead. A murmur ran through the crowd as people said, "He's dead." But Jesus took him by the hand and helped him to his feet, and he stood up.

If we all just believe in God and what he can do in our lives, we would all be better off. Vira believed in God and succeeded in what she was trying to accomplish. I was starting to see that I was not just going to be handed this opportunity; I had to earn it, something I was used to doing ever since I was a girl, and I was grateful for that. God encourages us to do good works.

What good is it, my brothers, if someone says he has faith but does not have works? Can that faith save him? If a brother or sister is poorly clothed and lacking in daily food, and one of you says to them, "Go in peace, be warmed and filled," without giving them the things needed for the body, what good is that? So also faith by itself, if it does not have works, is dead. But someone will say, "You have faith and I have works." Show me your faith apart from your works, and I will show you my faith by my works. You believe that God is one; you do well. Even the demons believe—and shudder! Do you want to be shown, you foolish person, that faith apart from works is useless? Was not Abraham our father justified by works when he offered up his son Isaac on the altar? You see that faith was active along with his works, and faith was completed by his works; and the Scripture was fulfilled that says, "Abraham believed God, and it was counted to him as righteousness"—and he was called a friend of God. You see that a person is justified by works and not by faith alone. And in the same way was not also Rahab the prostitute justified by works when she received the messengers and sent them out by another way? For as the body apart from the spirit is dead, so also faith apart from works is dead.

(James 2:14–26)

Thanks to Vira, I overcame my challenges in basic training and enhanced my spiritual journey with God. God takes his time to get to know all of us so that we have a better and more intimate relationship with him. He waits on us, he pushes us through our trials, he test our faith and motivates us through the process, and he speaks truth all out of his love for us so that we will not fail in life and end up in death. That is how passionate God is about his children, and through that selfless demonstration, we are to carry out his Word so others might come to know him just as he is, our Messiah.

I could not begin to compare with God, but I can live a life in his image, which we are all called to do as followers. So let's start with a short, sweet, young Hispanic girl named Carrie, who was homesick and at times doubted her capabilities. I considered her fully capable of handling basic training; she just needed someone to let her know that every once in a while.

The APFT was a challenge for most of the girls, and the thought of failing it made them feel bad about themselves. Self-doubt was their barrier, and that was Carrie's problem too. She would cry throughout the night and become really stressed out thinking that she might not pass the test. That gave me a great opportunity to speak with her about the gospel, and I shared with her the parable of the father whose son Jesus healed though the father had not believed Jesus could. Jesus cured the son and went even further to teach the father and others there a lesson: "Anything is possible for the one that believes." I wanted Carrie to lean on the father's response in the parable: "Help me in my unbelief." I wanted Carrie to know that God's miracles happen every day and to have faith in him.

The night before the APFT, I prayed that we would all pass. It was a hopeful prayer that most if not all the females would come out the next day feeling confident after they passed their APFT.

The next day, I saw the nervous tension going through the veins of the future soldiers surrounding me. Carrie came up to me for that last bit of encouragement, but before she could say a word, I said, "Carrie, I know you can do this. As long as you believe in God, you will never be disappointed. I can attest to that."

She thanked me for my words, but I knew she was doubting herself. I learned from competing in college that when I doubted God and lacked confidence, I barely made it around the track. Unfortunately, I believed in her capabilities more than she did, and because I could not take the test for her, she had to believe in herself if she wanted to pass the test. Vira on the other hand looked confident and ready to give it all she had; she believed in herself.

The drill sergeants sectioned us off into two rows per platoon. "Listen up, soldiers!" yelled the drill sergeant.

"Yes, Drill Sergeant!" we responded.

"Today, we will be conducting the APFT, which consist of push-ups, sit ups, and a two-mile run. First, you all will be completing as many correct push-ups as possible. Pay attention to the demonstration."

A drill sergeant began demonstrating how we soldiers were going to be graded on the push-up portion.

"Starting position is front leaning rest position. When the two minutes begin, you will make sure that your chest goes down toward the ground first being careful that your thighs do not hit the ground first. When you come back up, assure that your elbows lock, and then perform the next correct push-up. Your graders will be watching you closely. Does anyone have any questions?"

"No, Drill Sergeant!"

I was fifth in my line; Vera was first in the other line. I prayed that she would do well.

"Starting position … Get ready … Begin!"

I just knew that she would pass.

"Thirty seconds have passed," proclaimed the drill sergeant.

Vira was still going.

"A minute has passed."

Vira was still going, but by the time the drill sergeant called one minute and thirty seconds, she had dropped her knees. I was not sure if she had passed or failed.

One by one, each of us completed the first exercise. With an empty mind, I stepped up and completed the task with no issues.

When we did sit-ups, another soldier would hold our ankles. We started lying flat on our backs.

"The sit-up event measures the endurance of the abdominal and hip-flexor muscles," the drill sergeant explained.

On the command "Get set," with our fingers laced behind our heads, we sat up until we were vertical. We did as many as we could during our two minutes. At the end of each repetition, the grader stated only the number of sit-ups we had completed correctly.

All I could think about was Carrie. I prayed that she would not allow her anxiety to get the best of her especially since I could relate; sit-ups had always challenged me.

"As long as you make a continuous physical effort to sit, up the event will not be terminated. You may not use your hands or any other means to pull or push yourself up to the up, resting position or to hold yourself in the rest position ..." the sergeant explained.

When the drill sergeant told Carrie, "Get ready," I saw that she was sweating. That's when I knew she had psyched herself out. I hoped she had the confidence she'd need to do fifty-eight correct sit-ups in order to pass. When I glanced at her, she was at forty-two with a minute left. *Come on, Carrie! You can do it!* I thought.

By the time she had thirty seconds left, she had done forty-eight, and that was where she, exhausted, had to stop. I wept for her just as Jesus had wept for his friend in John 11.

> On his arrival, Jesus found that Lazarus had already been in the tomb for four days. Now Bethany was less than two miles from Jerusalem, and many Jews had come to Martha and Mary to comfort them in the loss of their brother. When Martha heard that Jesus was coming, she went out to meet him, but Mary stayed at home. "Lord," Martha said to Jesus, "if you had been here, my brother would not have died. But I know that even now God will give you whatever you ask." Jesus said to her, "Your brother will rise again."
>
> Martha answered, "I know he will rise again in the resurrection at the last day." Jesus said to her, "I am the resurrection and the life. The one who believes in me will live, even though they die; and whoever lives by believing in me will never die. Do you believe this?" "Yes, Lord," she replied, "I believe that you are the Messiah, the Son of God, who is to come into the world." After she had said this, she went back and called her sister Mary aside. "The

Teacher is here," she said, "and is asking for you."
When Mary heard this, she got up quickly and went
to him. Now Jesus had not yet entered the village,
but was still at the place where Martha had met
him. When the Jews who had been with Mary in
the house, comforting her, noticed how quickly she
got up and went out, they followed her, supposing
she was going to the tomb to mourn there. When
Mary reached the place where Jesus was and saw
him, she fell at his feet and said, "Lord, if you had
been here, my brother would not have died." When
Jesus saw her weeping, and the Jews who had come
along with her also weeping, he was deeply moved
in spirit and troubled. "Where have you laid him?"
he asked. "Come and see, Lord," they replied. Jesus
wept.

Most might say that Jesus wept because Lazarus was dead, which
is true, but you can also see that he wept because he saw the pain his
friends were in because of their brother's death. He wept with them
as I wept with my friend.

The last portion of the APFT was about to begin—the two-
mile run.

"On the command 'Go,' the clock will start …" a drill sergeant
said.

When my fellow runners in college would not do well, I would
pray to the Lord to ease their minds. One time, I started singing
out loud one of my favorite songs by the Christian artist Bethal,
"Come to Me," my go-to song that helps focus me on God and be
in his comfort. The song speaks about God being everything and
that he desires us to come to him because through the storm, there
is hope but only through him. God has us, and he won't let us go
as long as we allow him to fight for us and live in his presence. I

hoped Carrie knew that and that she chose to lean on God's truth instead of her own.

"Although walking is authorized, it is strongly discouraged …"

I felt that the military was always trying to discourage anyone from succeeding. However, if you thought about its tactics, they were similar to the Bible in a way. The Bible upholds truth and keeps us accountable if we read it for the truth it contains. The truth can be discouraging but only in the sense that God continues to mold us into whom he wants us to be. God does not mean to discourage us; he means to protect, motivate, and inspire us to share the gospel with others so that they will receive the same benefit we have and live in Christ. You gain more than you lose when you choose him, and after a while, you do not even consider it a loss.

"If you are physically helped in any way, for example, pulled, pushed, picked up and/or carried, or leave the designated running course for any reason, the event will be terminated …"

After the drill sergeant finished instructing us in all the specifics, he said, "Get ready … Get ready … Go!" and we were off. I ran with everything I had in me and ended with a success. I looked back and saw that Vira was not too far from finishing. She had passed her APFT. I saw that Carrie was not far from finishing either and was happy she would pass the run part of the test. Colossians 3:23 tells us, "Whatever you do, work at it with all your heart, as working for the Lord, not for human masters." After she crossed the line, I smiled at her to let her know that God and I were proud of her.

I took a deep breath and asked myself why I was blessed to be able to experience God's miracles, something so small to someone else actually being so big to God. She had finished. She had persevered. She had hope for her future. Watching God work in others' lives was the greatest thing I could imagine being a part of. It's the one thing that truly matters.

"Left! … Left! … Left!" The drill sergeants marched their platoons back to the drill hall floor. A loud voice shouted from a distance, "Company, attention … You have fifteen minutes to conduct personal hygiene and report back here in your ACUs (army combat uniform) … Fall out!"

We raced to our bay for quick showers and to change into our ACUs. I just despised these moments, but I made sure I was not late for formation and encouraged the others to not be late as well. I congratulated Vira and Carrie, and I looked to see if the others were doing everything they had to do to be successful. When someone was penalized for out-of-order behavior, I would join in in her punishment. If a drill sergeant gave a soldier push-ups to do, I would get down and do the same number of push-ups. I could not pass up an opportunity to demonstrate God's gospel.

Time seemed to go by fast in basic training. Before I knew it, we were back on the drill hall floor getting ready for the next briefing or the next thing we had to accomplish before being considered soldiers.

Our drill sergeants marched us down to the chow hall for breakfast. The day was just getting started, and so was training. I could go through all the things that were taught in basic training—cadences, army values, different combat courses, discipline, PG and APG responsibilities, countless one-minute showers, yelling and more yelling, insulting comments, push-up after push-up, competitions, second chances, handbooks with army regulations, the army song, the soldiers' creed, sleepless nights, fights in the bay, deaths of soldiers who could not handle the drill sergeants' criticism, on and on.

That night, I asked Carrie, "How are you doing?" and she began to cry.

"I don't believe I'm going to pass my APFT. I'm going to be a disappointment."

"You have to believe in yourself," I said. "You need to dedicate some time and practice."

"But I still don't believe I can do it!"

"God does, Carrie, and all he wants you to do is believe in that."

I started singing "Come to Me" and surrendered everything to God. That song brings me to my knees and repaints the picture of Christ shedding his blood for me and with his last breath asking God to forgive me. I never understood how anyone could love a stranger, and yet Christ demonstrated that so well. I wanted Carrie to feel like I felt and embrace Christ and be ignited by the Holy Spirit. Paul said it best when he wrote that he yearned for others to know God, and I wanted Carrie to know God's truth. When I saw her heart begin to fill, I knew the Lord would shine through her success despite her weaknesses.

Two weeks later, she had a chance to retake her APFT. With much confidence instilled in her by the grace of God, she would succeed I was sure. I praised God even before the miracle occurred. That night, I prayed for all who would be retaking the APFT.

I went about my day like normal as the morning turned into the afternoon. After the APFT redo ended, I went up to Carrie and asked her how she had done. "I passed!" she exclaimed giving all the glory to God. I was relieved. I wanted to remind her that God loved her as he did all his children and that he always shows up when we need him, but all I said was, "See?" I thanked the Lord for all he had done and was doing there. One step at a time, one miracle at a time.

Speaking of miracles, God was working through the lives of many females there, and I had the privilege and honor to be a part of it. Every step of basic training posed challenges for me, but one of the greatest was having to qualify on my M-16/M-4 weapon. I hoped I would never have to shoot anyone, but it was part of my training if I wanted to become a soldier. Perhaps the vision I had of myself was not the vision God had of me. Isaiah 55:8–9 tell us,

> "For my thoughts are not your thoughts, neither are your ways my ways," declares the Lord. "As the heavens are higher than the earth, so are my ways higher than your ways and my thoughts than your thoughts."

The day came for me to face this challenge. I felt okay, just a tad nervous. Cindy, a good friend, felt the same way. Almost every night, Cindy and I would talk about the difficulties of basic training and things back home that added to our stress. We weren't gossiping; we stayed focused on things to add to our prayer lists.

Cindy was committed to strengthening her relationship with Christ. As I shared the gospel with Cindy, we developed a close relationship; we were almost like sisters. Something about her made me comfortable; she was always so welcoming. Maybe it was her age—twenty-nine—and her wisdom that drew me closer to her. Despite her age, she wanted to fulfill her dream.

One day at the range, it was hot and cloudy due to the dust blowing around. The day was long, and we had to eat MREs, Meals Ready to Eat, throughout the day. They contained 3,000 calories of packaged foods compressed in a brown bag. Some of the food required water to prepare it; I enjoyed the crackers and cheese.

"Grace," Carrie said, "I'm worried. I've never held a weapon before, and I don't know if I can qualify."

I attempted to comfort her. "Carrie, remember when you felt you wouldn't pass your APFT because of the sit-ups but you did it?"

"Yes."

"Just as you had confidence that time, have confidence that you can qualify on your weapon."

"You're right," Carrie stated remembering what it had taken for her to pass the APFT. She regained the confidence she needed.

On the other hand, I was consumed with my own concerns because I had never fired a weapon before. The drill sergeants said that if we had not shot weapons before, it would be easier for us to learn how to do so correctly as opposed to soldiers who had shot weapons before and had developed their own habits.

Our drill sergeant taught us the four fundamentals of shooting our rifles: we had to have a steady position, spot the target, aim through the sights, and pull the trigger without improperly breathing while squeezing the trigger.

"Do I make myself clear?"

"Yes, Drill Sergeant!"

That was the seventh time one of the drill sergeants had explained to us how to properly prepare and shoot our weapons, but they also told us frightening stories about soldiers accidently killing other soldiers, which helped me understand why they kept repeating themselves on this subject.

Regardless, I was terrified. I didn't know exactly what to expect in spite of the instructions. Throughout college, I had been a hands-on learner. Instructions were not enough; I had to experience things to understand them.

We had to zero in our weapons, that is, make sure the sights were accurate by shooting five out of six rounds into a four-centimeter circle in the target.

"The M16A2 rifle has two adjustable sights front and rear. Elevation adjustments are made using the front sight, and elevation changes and wind age adjustments are made using the rear sight. The rear sight has an elevation knob with range indicators …"

I could not wrap my head around what the drill sergeant was saying. I was nervous and doubtful about myself. I could not do it. I was starting to be filled with a ton of doubt, and I needed reassurance.

"To adjust windage or move the strike of the round, turn the windage knob …"

The more nervous I became, the harder it was for me to understand the drill sergeant.

"Carefully aim and fire each shot of a three-shot group at the circle on the silhouette. If your shot group is not within the circle on the silhouette, use the squares on the target …"

All this was way too much to try and take in in one day. I had wished that the drill sergeant would not be so repetitive, but then, I wanted more instruction. I was all over the place in my thoughts.

Our sergeant would put quarters on top of our rifles; we were supposed to squeeze the trigger gently enough that the quarter wouldn't fall off when we fired the rifle.

The drill sergeants lined us up and gave us ammo as we prepared to qualify our weapons. This was the first day of two, and my goal was to qualify the first day and get it over with.

I saw Cindy coming off the range wearing her protective eyewear. She looked irritated. She passed by me, and I asked, "Did you qualify?"

With annoyance, she said, "Naw, girl, I did not, and it's hot. I'm ready to go." She went to eat in the shade.

"Hurry! Move down the line!" The drill sergeants always yelled, but for some reason, their words were piercing my veins and filling me with fear. I was moments away from attempting to qualify.

"You are going to be shooting out of lane nine. Make sure you point your muzzle down range. Go!"

"Yes, Drill Sergeant!" I said.

"Walk, private! Move with a purpose!"

I picked up my pace with my muzzle pointing down range and my ammo jiggling in my pocket, and I arrived at my lane and stood waiting for instructions.

"Soldiers, get in a comfortable, prone, supported position …"

That position provided the most stable platform for shooting (see figures 3–8). Upon entering the position, the soldier adds or removes dirt, sandbags, or other supports to adjust for his or her height. He then faces the target, executes a half-face to his firing side, and leans forward until his chest is against the firing-hand corner of the position. He places the rifle handguard in a V formed by the thumb and fingers of his nonfiring hand, and rests the nonfiring hand on the material (sandbags or berm) to the front of the position. The soldier places the stock butt in the pocket of his firing shoulder and rests his firing elbow on the ground outside the position.

My helmet kept sliding down over my eyes, which blocked my view of the moving targets.

"Lock and load … Take the selective switch off safe, and keep an eye out for your lane … Begin firing when ready!"

My mind was racing. I was sweating. Anxiety took hold of me. By the time the first target came up, I had forgotten all the fundamentals.

"Cease fire! Are there any alibis?"

Alibis were rounds that a soldier had not been able to fire due to a weapon jamming, too few in the magazine, and so on. Range control held up a green sign proclaiming that there were no alibis.

"Lock and load your next magazine … Take a comfortable, unsupported prone position …"

This firing position (figures 3–9) offers another stable firing platform for engaging targets. To assume this position, the soldier faces his target, spreads his feet a comfortable distance apart, and drops to his knees. Using the butt of the rifle as a pivot, the firer rolls onto his nonfiring side, placing the nonfiring elbow close to the side of the magazine. He places the rifle butt in the pocket formed by the firing shoulder, grasps the pistol grip with his firing hand, and lowers the firing elbow to the ground. The rifle rests in the V formed by the thumb and fingers of the nonfiring hand. The soldier adjusts the position of his firing elbow until his shoulders are about level, and pulls back firmly on the rifle with both hands. To complete the position, he obtains a stock weld and relaxes, keeping his heels close to the ground.

"Take the selective switch off safe, and keep an eye out for your lane. Begin firing when ready."

I took a deep breath and saw the first target pop up, but I was not sure I hit it. I panicked when I realized I was not hitting any of the targets. Though I knew I had not qualified with the first two magazines, I was determined to give it my all with my last one. I aimed and I shot, and before I knew it, I was done.

The drill sergeant read off the scores, and I had hit fifteen out of forty targets; I thought I was not far from qualifying. I was directed off the range to wait under the tents until it was time for me to try again.

I must have tried six times that day, and the highest I got was twenty. The drill sergeants were trying everything to help me succeed. I went back and rezeroed my weapon. The more attempts I took, the more tired I became, but the more faith I had in God. I was hopeful the entire way through.

> But he said to me, My grace is sufficient for you, for my power is made perfect in weakness. Therefore I will boast all the more gladly about my weaknesses, so that Christ's power may rest on me. That is why, for Christ's sake, I delight in weaknesses, in insults, in hardships, in persecutions, in difficulties. For when I am weak, then I am strong.
>
> (2 Corinthians 12:9–10)

I'd overcome challenges all my life, and this was another I'd handle. After my restless spirit had decided to rest in Christ, I knew I could do it. It seemed that God had painted a picture in my head, but it was in black and white rather than in color; I was the black while everything around me was the white. It seemed that even if I trusted in Christ, I'd end up flat on my face. Athletes stumble. Children can feel all alone even at home. Challenges are hard to face, and we can find ourselves buried in our own false truth, and we can deprive ourselves of being able to live.

God is the answer, the solution, and in him, we achieve victory. I have learned that life is what we make of it and how we define it, and I chose to accept Christ. My God loves me, and whatever life brings to me, I'll be ready to take on my challenges. I will not have all the answers, but I will have just enough to get through any obstacle whether it is the death of my brother, the loss of my mother, or never having known the true face of my biological father.

I know now what I have and what people aren't able to give me. I hope that the Lord will free me from any bitterness that I might hold deep inside me because I feel as though I'm lacking something that I do not need. The Lord has always been extremely generous to me. Sure, I wish some things in my life were different, but I know I have more than many people do, and that is more than enough.

People had purposely put me down to lift themselves up, but it was my time to stand on top and be firm on my own feet. I needed to qualify on this day if I wanted to serve my country as well as myself.

"Pull your bolt back …"

My drill sergeant walked next to me, confident that I could do this. I looked up at the sky and whispered to God that it was time and that I knew he was right there with me. I walked to lane nine and readied myself.

One of my drill sergeants was lying down next to me, encouraging me every step of the way. "You have this; just remember the fundamentals," he said.

Something was different about that; he was not yelling at me but rather talking to me like he believed I could do this. It started to rain. I loaded my magazine and took a deep breath.

"Place the selective switch from safe to semi, and watch your lane …"

I was focused. With every breath, I moved from one target to the next. I was inspired every time I shot a target down and my drill sergeant said, "Hit!" I had to stay focused.

"Hit!"

I was trusting in the Lord with all my strength. I knew God would not have brought me this far just to have me turn back now.

"Hit!"

"Cease fire! Lock and clear all weapons!"

I knew I was not alone. I looked up to the sky and felt that what was left of my brother came down and was standing next to me. A person never leaves you but rather carries on his or her life somewhere far greater than earth. That's heaven. Certain moments bring you closer to those who are no longer on this earth, and often, it happens right when you need to feel their presence the most. They're like guardian angels hovering over you and encouraging you. No matter what we go through, God finds a way to provide us with what we need to get through it. I prepared to say goodbye to my struggles and focus on God, who never gave up on me; he loved me enough to send his son to die for me. I dug into hope and rested in my faith.

> Love is patient, love is kind. It does not envy, it does not boast, it is not proud. It does not dishonor others, it is not self-seeking, it is not easily angered, it keeps no record of wrongs. Love does not delight in evil but rejoices with the truth. It always protects, always trusts, always hopes, always perseveres.
>
> (1 Corinthians 13:4–8)

It was over. My drill sergeant and I listened to the drill sergeant in the tower call out the results. I was ready for whatever the drill sergeant in the tower would say. I had to get twenty-three out of forty.

"Lane two, twenty-three! ... Lane eight, thirty-five! ... Lane nine, twenty-eight!"

I had qualified! My drill sergeant and I shouted with joy. The struggle was over.

After that, everything else fell into place. It would not be long before I would graduate. Basic training was the first thing I accomplished after the death of my brother; with God's strength, anything is possible.

I got on the bus after graduating, remembering when I wasn't sure I would make it, but I had. That was when I just let it all out; tears streamed from my eyes. I finally gave myself the chance to mourn for everything I had lost and to rejoice for everything I had gained. It was a profound moment.

My life had been difficult at times. I felt that I had been walking through fire for a long time, trying not to get burned and hoping that the smoke would clear. I finally learned that being intimate with God had freed me from the hot fire and the suffocating smoke. With God, I am able to walk through anything.

> But now, this is what the Lord says—
> he who created you, Jacob,
> he who formed you, Israel:
> Do not fear, for I have redeemed you;
> I have summoned you by name; you are mine.
> When you pass through the waters,
> I will be with you;
> and when you pass through the rivers,
> they will not sweep over you.
> When you walk through the fire,
> you will not be burned;
> the flames will not set you ablaze.
> —Isaiah 43:1–2

AFTERWORD

Life still continues for me. I now firmly believe that no matter what I go through, if God's hands are in it, I can get through it. These trials are no more than that—trials. They are not my curses or my identity; they are blessings and the vital ingredients of my beautiful dish, my testimony.

Robert Frost, one of my favorite authors, wrote, "Two roads diverged in a wood, and I, I took the one less traveled by, and that has made all the difference." It made all the difference to make the choices I've made. If I were to pass on tomorrow, I would be proud of my decisions despite some of them being mistakes. My life could have gone either way, but I chose to follow the guidance of God, which led me to a wonderful life. Yes, at times, it was filled with sorrow and pain, but it is filled with God's truth and love. My faith gets me through everything.

I'm still mourning my brother's death, but I have developed wonderful relationships with wonderful friends, and I've discovered new things as well.

My older brother is schizoaffective, and my biological mother was found alive. Sadly, just recently my sister was killed while trying to support and help one of her close friends. All in all, no matter what obstacles continue to be known in my life, I stand firm with God in order to overcome them.

About fifteen years ago, I would not have been able to say this, but it is not about what you go through but how you go through it. I know there is no specific way to get through things, but if you want to come out of it on the other side, the best tool and guide is God's truth. I've loved, I've laughed, and I've lost, but most important, I've persevered, and because of that, I have a chance at life.

A wise person once told me that he believed God does not intend bad things to happen but works through those bad things to show that he is God. Yes, I have walked through fire and inhaled smoke, but the beauty of this journey is that I was never alone.